BEER

A GAUGE FOR ENTHUSIASTS

BEER

A GAUGE FOR ENTHUSIASTS

GREG DUNCAN POWELL

MURDOCH BOOKS

A NOTE FROM GREG

It's been pointed out before that there are 24 beers in a case and 24 hours in the day — spooky serendipity or the natural order of the universe? It's very probably the latter. Beer enthusiasts can measure time, distance and even life itself by the amount of beer that can be consumed over a given period. This is a 150-beer book, which in beer-time translates to 18 nights at the pub, about 3000 km or a month of time on the planet.

Unfortunately, when you're tasting and writing from the discomfort of your tasting lab rather than the mullioned snug of the pub, beer-time runs slow and the whole drinking process takes a lot longer and is a more arduous task than it sounds. While it might be the dying wish of many to sit down in front of 150 beers, believe me, you can have too much of a good thing. One positive is that you do get to look very closely at the Australian beerscape. And how has it changed! Beer consumption is the lowest since 1960, but that doesn't mean that Australians are less interested in beer, on the contrary, they have never been more engaged. There are a batch of beers and breweries that weren't around a decade ago, brand loyalty has gone out the window and drinkers are actually questioning what they drink!

Of course, some things haven't changed. Some brewers are still bemused by the idea that a drinks writer, such as I, would have the temerity to critique their product — and actually ask for a sample to taste. For some, supplying their beer for the purpose of tasting has proved an impossible task. When all attempts failed, the beer for the tasting was procured in the time-honoured fashion that most drinkers use — with money from a shop.

But at closing time, with all 150 beers tasted and the empties in the recycling, I'd have to state that beer-wise, we've never been in better shape. There's plenty of choice, the ale/lager imbalance is being redressed and there have never been so many good beers in our land.

Cheers

Greg Duncan Powell

CONTENTS

DO YOU REALLY NEED TO KNOW ABOUT BEER?

It's simple isn't it? You buy it, chill it, remove the cap, open your mouth, pour it inside, swallow and repeat as necessary. At least that's how it used to be. Beer drinking wasn't something you read about – it was something you did instinctively. But it's a different world now. Today, it's expected that a drinker know at least a little bit about their chosen beverage.

This is as it should be – knowledge is power and more knowledge means better beer. Not so long ago, the average male grew up drinking the same beer from cradle to grave. He had nothing to measure its quality against and was bound to think it tasted good. In NSW, they drank Tooheys or Resch's and were compelled to hate the other brand. Victorians drank the Carlton and United Breweries (CUB) products. In SA it was Westend or Southwark, while the smart ones consumed Coopers. In WA it was Swan or Emu Bitter, the Queenslanders were four-exed and in Tasmania, Boags or Cascade were consumed along geographical lines, depending on which half of the island you lived.

With the brewery buyouts of the 1980s came a sort of beer federalisation. State borders were crossed and we all got to know how good the Tasmanians had had it – and how the Queenslanders had suffered.

But it wasn't just internal beer borders that opened. Bottle shops were flooded with immigrants from far-off lands that tasted different to (and better than) the local product – proper pilsners, bitter English ales, funky Belgian beers. Boutique brews sprang up that actually tasted like they were made from malt and hops. Aussie beer was given a good kick in the pants and breweries started to improve their game. Premium beers emerged and another type of beer drinker was born – one who wasn't eternally loyal to one brand, but chose the beer depending on what he (or she) felt like. The whole revolutionary notion that there could be a different beer for every occasion gradually began to take shape.

Now we face a situation where – strange as it may seem – there is almost too much beer: foreign beers that no-one has ever heard of, a micro-brewery in every town and megaglomerates like Foster's and Lion Nathan releasing a you-beaut new brew onto a sodden marketplace every month.

So what is a drinker to do? The first thing is to arm oneself against the barrage of marketing bullshit that is rained down in the name of beer. The second is to keep the palate tuned, honed, fit and ready for battle against insurgent brews; and the third is to read this book.

A SHORT HISTORY OF BREWING

Given the importance of beer to Australian life and culture, most drinkers know precious little about its place in history. We get the hagiographic stuff in beer ads, but the background and evolution of the first proper bottom-fermented lager, or the effect Louis Pasteur had upon brewing, is not something you learn about at school. So, for all those who missed out on this important historical information, while learning about the Magna Carta or Captain Cook, following is a short history of beer.

It was around 15,000 years ago that humans settled down and began to plant grain. It's reasonable to assume that as men and women got to grips with bread and starch, they would have discovered its fermentable properties too. But the first actual mention of beer in human civilisation doesn't occur until 9000 years later – around 4000 BC in Sumeria. According to the legend, the Sumerians discovered brewing by chance. A loaf of bread falls into some water, there are a few yeast cells floating about in the atmosphere and – voila! – beer (of a sort). The Sumerians probably discovered beer this way because their brew was made from baked bread, not milled or malted grain, and was thought to be the work of a 'brewing goddess'. A hymn to the goddess describes the 'exhilarated, wonderful, blissful' effects that come from drinking beer. It's a similar intoxication to what beer drinkers enjoy today. But the drinking of this 'beer' was very different – filtration and clarity were not priorities in Sumerian brewing, and beer straws were used to suck the liquid from the sludge. Drinkers would gather around an earthenware vessel full of beer with their drinking straws, being careful not to disturb the sediment too much.

The *Epic of Gilgamesh* is one of the oldest surviving literary works – dating back to Ancient Mesopotamia – and features beer as its central protagonist. The story is about Enkidu, a bestial primitive man, who ate grass and had the ability to milk wild animals. Enkidu wanted to test his strength against the warrior king Gilgamesh. Gilgamesh being a little worried about the strength of this upstart challenger and his skill with lactating fauna, sent a prostitute to spy on Enkidu in order to learn his strengths, weaknesses and his innermost secrets. Enkidu spent a fulfilling week with the lady and, while not making love, she taught him a little about civilisation and introduced him to some comestibles that weren't based on the dairy products of wild beasts – she gave Enkidu bread and beer and apparently said 'Eat the bread Enkidu, as it belongs to life. Drink also beer, as it is the custom of the land'. Enkidu drank seven cups of beer and his heart soared. The story says that 'In this condition, he washed himself and became a human being'.

Contemporary readers might suggest that this is the wrong way around – beer returns man to his primitive, ape-like state. But the reason that drunkenness was synonymous with civility is because intoxication wasn't frowned upon. To the Sumerians, drunkenness was the effect of divine spirits inhabiting the body – a theory that makes being pissed seem so much more dignified and spiritual.

After the Babylonians invaded Sumeria, they took the beer recipe back to Babylon and from there it spread to Egypt. The Egyptians made beer from bread dough and added flavourings that ranged from juniper to coriander and even saffron. This was a pre-hops world.

The beer versus wine divide, which still persists today, actually took hold in Ancient Rome. Beer was associated with Barbarians, even though the Romans introduced brewing to them. Ale was the beverage consumed on the edges of the Empire and the colder bits of Europe, where wine wasn't grown or available. Tacitus, a Roman snob of the highest order and historian of the German tribes, puts it like this: 'To drink, the Teutons have a horrible brew fermented from barley or wheat, a brew which has only a very far removed similarity to wine.'

A Nordic writer and beer drinker was happy to assign wine to the gods and beer to mortals. At that time, both drinks would have been pretty awful and in various stages of going off – the wine, vinegary, and the beer, cloudy and flat.

During the Dark Ages that followed the collapse of the Roman Empire, monasteries kept the light on and the wine and beer flowing. There was a very good reason why monks devoted so much time to both brewing and viticulture. These were beverages that were not forbidden during fasts and the monks could indulge themselves to a fairly immoderate degree. A Benedictine monk was allowed to consume five litres of beer a day! In Sumerian terms that meant that a monk could be totally inhabited by the divine spirit without breaking the Benedictine code. The link between monks and brewing is ancient and strong. In fact, Munich, or Munchen, the beer capital of the world, means 'monk' and the tradition still continues in Belgium today.

There is plenty of conjecture about when a hop cone was first lobbed into a brew. Some historians suggest that monks in a Brabant monastery in the 8th century were the first, but legend attributes the first gift of hops to a woman. She was Hildegard of Bingen and was abbess at a convent near the Rhine in Germany. The story goes that she gave her imprimatur to a brew that was made using hops, which suggests that the practice was already known.

Like most great revolutions, the spread of hops took time. In northern Europe, ale made from fermented grain was called 'gruit', and was consumed unadulterated by hops but was flavoured with a multitude of herbs. The big gruit interests saw the danger in this new beer and resisted it for all they were worth. Holland in particular tried to hold out against the Hamburg (hopped) beer, instituting a multitude of import laws against it – all to no avail. By the end of the 14th century, the prohibitions were over. Gruit was gone and Holland had embraced hops.

Much the same battle was fought in Britain. The English developed a taste for hopped beer fighting wars in the Low Countries and brought the hop plant back to Britain, where it was first planted in 1428. In Britain, hopped beer and ale co-existed for a time despite Henry VIII's attempts to forbid beer brewed with hops. By 1550, England was a land of hopped ale, and only the very northern bits of Scotland held out with brewing gruit.

While the preservative, anti-bacterial properties of hops allowed for more stable brews at lower alcohol levels, brewing was still a hit or miss business. Brewing relied on wild wind-born yeasts, which tended to be a bit chancy. In hot weather, and sometimes for no apparent reason at all, the yeast would go berserk, turning the brew sour. This is why most successful brewing was done in the cooler months. The next big beer revolution came with the studies on microbiology by Louis Pasteur. Louis discovered that the brewing goddess was, in fact, yeast – a living organism that converted sugar into alcohol, but could also be contaminated by other microorganisms.

Towards the end of the 18th century, Louis Pasteur's work inspired Emil Hansen of the Carlsberg Brewery in Denmark to single out a pure yeast cell. This allowed for the invention of lager – and possibly one of the greatest moments in human history.

In the German language, 'lager' means 'to store'. The theory goes that the Germans were storing beer in caves with ice for summer-time consumption (when brewing was suspended because of the risk of spoilage) and accidentally hit upon the effect of cool, slow, bottom fermentation. Lagers were made almost

accidentally by slowing down the fermenting process via the coolness of the caves, which made the yeast drop to the bottom of the brew and out of the way of passing bacteria. However, these were still dark beers made with heavily roasted malt.

A confluence of accidents contrived to create the world's first pale lager, as we know it. In most breweries, the way the malt was dried was quite harsh and invariably meant roast malt and dark coloured beer, but in the town of Pilsen in 1842, Josef Groll used malt that had been dried a bit more gently and hence made a more pale brew (some even claim that it was accidentally not dried at all). The local barley also happened to be low in protein, which helped the brew's clarity. There was plenty of the local strain of hops, Saaz, and the local water, which was very soft – meaning that the colour wasn't leached from the malt as happens with hard water.

Almost at the same time, the use of glassware was becoming more common, which meant that the glories of the new beer could be properly appreciated.

From Pilsen, the new beer spread to Dortmund, which began brewing pale lager in 1873, and by 1894 the Spaten brewery in Munich was brewing pale lagers. However, brewing was still a seasonal occupation and lager brewing was limited by refrigeration technology. Breweries were the largest industrial consumers of ice, but in 1895 German Carl von Linde created a way of making liquid oxygen, which made industrial refrigeration available to breweries. Lager-brewing technology spread to beer-drinking nations – and world domination soon followed.

'WORTS' AND ALL –
WHAT'S REALLY IN
YOUR BEER?

Beer is a bit like bread — there are three basic ingredients and a billion ways to bake (or brew) it. Bread is flour, water and yeast, with seasoning of some sort — usually salt. Beer is grain, yeast and water, with seasoning — usually hops. They're simple ingredients that can be combined in different ways to make very different things. A bagel and a loaf of Buttercup are as far apart as a stubby of VB and an exotic Bock. Given good tools and decent ingredients, the brewer, like the baker, is only limited by his or her imagination.

Barley

You can make beer out of Uncle Tobys rolled oats if you choose, but the grain that is the most suited for brewing is barley. Barley seems to have been put on this earth by a loving God to produce thirst-slaking ale. Even the barley husk acts as a natural filter in the first stage of brewing.

But barley's most advantageous characteristics come from malting. Malting is the process of germinating grain and then drying it. The malting process helps change the sugars in the grain so that they can be fermented. To get a bit technical for a moment, barley has a high diastatic power, which means that it is high in enzymes that can convert starch into sugar or maltose. Other grains can be malted but usually don't have the enzymes to do the job on the starches to the same effect. The malting process involves soaking the grain until the little germinating tails appear and then drying it. This is where tweaks to style, flavour and colour are produced. Like coffee beans, the amount of heat applied to the malt affects flavour and colour. Of the multitude of different malts a brewer can choose, there are generally four main types:

Pilsner malt — The basis for Germanic-style lagers. Light in colour and flavour.
Crystal malt — A halfway point between dark-roasted malt and pilsner malt. It adds colour and flavour, but can be used for lighter beers.
Munich malt — Slightly darker and more roasted than pilsner malt.
Chocolate malt — As the name suggests, this is a dark, heavily roasted malt and adds those accompanying chocolatey, roasted flavours.

Water

When you think about it, 95% of a 5.0%-alcohol by volume beer is water, so it's pretty important. It's so important, in fact, that brewers don't even call it 'water'. Inside the brewery, water is called 'liquor' — and it's not just what ends up in the bottle that affects the flavour. The whole brewing process uses swimming pools of H_2O, and the hardness and purity of the water affects the way that the malt ferments, and the colour and flavour of the final brew. This is the reason that breweries were traditionally sited close to clean sources of water. These days, river frontage is not so important — modern breweries just adjust their water to their needs, balancing pH and filtering, to prepare it for the brew.

Yeast

Yeast is, in ignition terms, the spark plug for the brew. Brewing yeast is a unicellular fungus — a species of budding yeast, meaning it increases by buds and then becomes other yeast cells. *Saccharomyces cerevisiae*, as it is called, is the granddaddy brewing yeast, but there are innumerable subspecies of this yeast used in brewing — one of which is the lager yeast known as *Saccharomyces carlsbergensis*, named after the brewery that originally isolated it. As with wine, the use of different yeasts can add different characteristics to the final brew. Attenuation – the efficiency with which the yeast converts sugar to alcohol – differs from strain to strain, and some yeasts perform better at a certain pH and alcoholic strength. Some yeasts add very little or no flavour to a beer, while others give secondary characteristics which can be good or bad depending on what the brewer is after. Yeast-derived flavours fall into three main groups: phenols, which are generally perceived as spicy notes; esters, which give fruity flavours; and diacetyls, which can give beers a woody taste.

Hops

Imagine cooking without spices, salt or pepper – that's pretty much how beer would be without hops. Hops have been around for millennia. They're a part of the same family as cannabis and hemp, and were around in Babylon during the Jewish captivity. The Roman, Pliny, mentions them in his natural history. According to him, the hops grew wild among willows 'like a wolf among sheep' – hence the Latin name for hops, *lupulus*.

Hops grew wild but were relatively difficult to cultivate. The first mention of an actual hop garden is in 736 AD in Hallertau, Germany, which gives its name to a famous Noble hop. Like most smelly botanical species, there was much superstition, but also some correct applications. Insomnia in pre-pharmaceutical times was sometimes treated with hop cones inserted into the pillowcase – and indeed the female buds have a high methylbutanol content, which has been shown to have a calming effect.

It is the way that hops interact with yeast and fermenting beer that is most interesting. Hop cones are extremely resinous, sticky things

that contain two sorts of acids – alpha and beta. Alpha acids are mildly anti-bacterial and the main contributors to bitterness and flavour – especially when they're boiled with the wort; beta acids add aroma but not bitterness.

A QUICK GUIDE TO HOPS

Admiral – An English bittering hop used in some English ales.

Amarillo Gold – It sounds like exotic cannabis, but is in fact a mid-range alpha hop.

Brewer's Gold – This is a British bittering high-range alpha hop developed in 1919.

Cascade – American aromatic hop developed in the 1950s from Fuggles and a Russian variety, Serebrianker.

Challenger – An English hop introduced in 1972 with some pine and citrus notes.

Chinook – An aromatic American hop with a tropical perfume.

Crystal – An aromatic hop bred from Hallertau and Cascade.

First Gold – A dwarf hop with the character of Goldings.

Fuggles – Famous cuddly-named English-ale hop which dates from the late 1800s.

Golden Nuggets – A bittering hop sometimes just referred to as 'Nuggets'.

Goldings – Popular English aromatic hop that dates back to the 1700s.

Hallertau – Named after the town in Bavaria – it is one of the Noble aromatic hops.

Hersbrucker – One of the most famous and aristocratic of the lager hops. Gives European class to a basic lager.

Liberty – Recently developed Hallertau cross which is resistant to downy mildew.

Lublin – Named after the city in eastern Poland, it is Poland's own Hersbrucker.

Magnum – A bittering aromatic hop bred in 1980.

Millennium – A bittering hop and cousin of Golden Nuggets.

Mount Hood – A soft American variety developed from Hallertau.

Nelson Sauvin – A relatively new variety developed in Nelson, New Zealand, it was released for commercial production in 2000. This hop has almost sauvignon blanc like characteristics – hence the name.

Newport – An American bittering hop.

Northdown – Dual purpose hop from England developed in the 1970s, with bitterness and a soft aroma.

Northern Brewer – A cross-Atlantic English and American blend.

Pacific Gem – A bittering hop harking from New Zealand.

Perle – Floral German dual-purpose hop, often used in combination with other hops.

Pioneer – English aromatic hop related to Herald.

Pride of Ringwood – Famous Australian hop. First used in 1965 when it was the highest-range alpha acid hop in the world – and still used extensively in Australian lagers.

Progress – Developed in the 1960s in Britain, it is often used as a substitute for Fuggles.

Saaz – Famous Noble hop from the Czech Republic with recognisable clean perfume.

Santiam – American aromatic hop that has parentage that includes Hallertau and Cascade.

Saphire – An aromatic hop bred to replace Hallertau, which is particularly susceptible to disease and pests.

Select – German disease-resistant Hallertau and Spalter pale-lager variety, developed in the early 1990s.

Simcoe – American hop with a distinct tropical aroma.

Spalter – Noble German hop in the class of Hallertau and Saaz.

Sterling – A cross between Saaz and Mount Hood hops.

Strisselspalt – French hop from Alsace, used in lager, most notably the celebrated brew, Kronenbourg 1664.

Styrian Goldings – A European version of Fuggles, which is used in Belgian ales.

Tardif de Bourgogne – Aromatic French hop from Burgundy, which is used in lagers.

Target – Cousin of Goldings.

Tradition – Yet another easier-to-grow version of Hallertau.

Tettnanger – One of the Noble German hops and in the class of Saaz and Hallertau.

Ultra – Aromatic hop bred in the 1980s from a cross of the two Nobles, Hallertau and Saaz.

Vanguard – Another Hallertau variant.

Warrior – New American bittering hop.

Willamette – American variant of Fuggles.

Zeus – American aromatic high-alpha hop with noticeable bitterness.

ADDITIVES IN BEER

I have a strange facility for remembering beer ads. With the tune in my head I can still see side-burned blokes from the '70s pouring beers and sucking on cans. Invariably the themes eulogised blokedom – *'With a right arm of iron and a taste for good cheer, he's a real expert drinker, Courage Draught is his beer.'* Then there was the Reschs Pilsener ad from the '80s – *'Belt your beer down, you're with your mates. Knock 'er back son, 'ppreciate.'* And a host of versions of *'It's the beer we drink here',* depending on which state you were in. The beer ad genre is laddish, sometimes funny, but never informative. I can't think of a single one that bragged about the ingredients or the brewing process.

In the 'old days' beer was beer – and what it constituted was neither here nor there. It's only recently that drinkers have started to question what they pour down their throats. Given that we consume about 100 litres of beer per capita per annum, it's perfectly reasonable to ask what's in it. Carlton reacted against this new interest in the brewing process by trying to mock it in its advertising. *'We use only the most attractive yeast',* the ads boasted, and *'Our beer is made in big shiny things'.* The joke fell flat – we are in a new era.

The growth of boutique brews that can legitimately claim 'no preservatives or additives' on the tin makes us look critically at the labels of those that don't make the same claims. What is in those beers? Well, as with most mass-produced consumables, there are various industry short cuts that make the whole process more predictable, efficient and economically viable. For beer, that means additives – see the page opposite for some of the favourites.

Adjuncts

Adjuncts are the things that go into beer that breweries are not inclined to list on the label. Since the Reinheitsgebot of 1516 – the Bavarian purity law that claimed that anything that wasn't made from hops, malt, water and yeast wasn't beer – adjuncts have been perceived as evil. In the brewing lexicon, 'adjuncts' are unmalted grains and sugars: rice, corn, oats, wheat and cane sugar. There are many reasons they can be added to beer. They can add or dilute the taste, they can affect the physical properties of the beer (a little wheat can help head retention), but more often than not, the starch of choice is chosen for economic reasons. Malted grain is expensive, which is why in rice-growing regions like Asia, rice is the adjunct of choice. In corn-growing countries like the US, it's corn; and in countries that grow sugar cane, like Australia, it's cane sugar.

The long and short of labelling is that if there's no guarantee that the beer only contains malt, hops, water and yeast you can bet there are adjuncts and additives in there.

Propylene glycol alginate – an emulsifying product found in everything from ice cream to sexual lubricant that helps the foam and head retention in beer

Silicone – used during fermentation as an anti-foam device so that the tanks can be filled up without precious beer foaming out of the top

Amyloglucosidase – turns non-fermentable sugars into fermentable sugars

Betaglucanase – acts on the starches and speeds up the fermentation process

Rhoiso-alpha acids – gives the hopping a boost

Protease – an enzyme that helps convert proteins

Ammonia caramel – brown colouring similar to the stuff they put in Coke

Sulphur dioxide – (commonly known as preservative 220) used in everything from dried fruit to wine to maintain colour and stop oxidisation

HOW LAGER IS MADE – A TEN-STAGE PROCESS

1. Milling
Malted barley is crushed in a mill to form grist ready for the mash.

2. Mashing
The milled barley and hot water are mixed together to form a sort of porridge.

3. Lautering
Lauter is German for 'filter' and is a crucial part of the process – without it we'd all be drinking fermented barley porridge. The liquid, or 'wort', is drained from the husks, which go off to become feed for ruminant animals.

4. Boiling
The 'green' wort (as it's called before the addition of yeast) is boiled and a 'gift' of hops – or at least hop pellets – is added. During this boiling stage, much of the bitterness and aroma are extracted. With most Australian brews, this is also when cane sugar is added.

5. Whirlpooling
This is a specialised tank, or the brew kettle in smaller breweries, which, by a whirlpooling action, allows the sediment and hop residue to collect in the centre. Known in the wonderful language of brewing as 'trub', it goes off to become pig feed.

6. Cooling
The cleaned-up wort is then cooled through a heat exchanger to about 10°C.

7. Fermentation
Yeast is added to the brew and oxygen is often dissolved into the wort to help the yeast work. The brew starts fermenting – turning the sugars in the wort to alcohol and carbon dioxide. After about four or five days, all the sugars have been fermented into alcohol and without food (i.e. sugar), the yeast dies and sinks to the bottom of the fermenter. In commercial breweries, the fermenters are cone-shaped and the yeast sinks into the pointy bit of the cone where it can be pumped out. It then goes off to become everyone's favourite breakfast spread – Vegemite.

8. Maturation
The new beer, or 'green beer' as it's called, is now stored in lagering tanks for as long as ten days at a shade below freezing. This allows many of the nasties and proteins to precipitate out of the beer, for the flavours to coalesce and for carbon dioxide to become locked in the beer.

9. Filtration
Beer is filtered through various forms of filtration, including diatomaceous earth and pad filters. The carbonation for the particular style is also adjusted at this point. The clear beer is now called 'bright beer'.

10. Packaging
The beer is now ready for packaging in keg, bottle, stubby or can.

THE RIGHT BEER FOR THE OCCASION

'You can get it any old how, matter of fact I've got it now!' Remember that legendary line? In that tedious ad, thirsts are acquired in many different ways — but the recommended cure is always the same. It's Victoria Bitter taken refrigerated and orally. We all accept now that this is wrong. Not the drinking part, but the VB part.

Back when the late John Mellion put his voice to that ad, it was a 'one beer fits all' scenario — and a request for the beer menu in the local pub was akin to asking for a punch in the head. The only customising available to the one-brand drinker was to dial the fridge up a bit, choose a stubby or can and drink it with or without the stubby holder. Some brands even gave the drinker the luxury of choosing between a 250ml 'throw-down', a stubby or a long neck. They were many different ways of doing essentially the same thing.

This is patently wrong. No single brand of beer can satisfy the multitude of beer-drinking occasions that life throws up — if you'll excuse that expression. It's a fact of life that certain qualities in certain beers shine when consumed after specific activities. Matching the beer to the beer thirst has real taste benefits — and a quiver of favourite brews is necessarily to get maximum pleasure from beer consumption.

The mowing-the-lawn thirst

You've been pushing a Victa through stubborn kikuyu – and maybe had to rake it up too. Even if you've been luxuriating on a ride-on, the thirst is similar, if a little less intense. It's driven by heat, the aroma of cut grass, the vibrations, noise and exhaust from the mower, and physical activity. For this sort of thirst the ideal beer is a lager – very cold, quite crisp and easy to throw down. It's a particularly satisfying thirst to slake as, job done, you reward yourself with a coldie surveying the lawn-scape you've just created.

The surfing (or swimming-in-the-sea) thirst

This kind of thirst is brought about by being immersed in the sea until the ends of the fingers have gone wrinkly. The mouth and taste buds become marinated in brine and, just as a salty chip has a special affinity with beer, so does a swimmer who has been pickled. This particular thirst seems to favour beers that are particularly heavy-handed in the hop department.

The I-need-something-else thirst

This one is fairly unique to the wine industry and usually occurs after a huge wine tasting or a dinner that's gone on way too long, or both. The palate has effectively been poisoned by wine and food and needs to be revived by a cleansing ale. In this case something crisp yet bold enough to awake the palate is required.

The no-thirst thirst

You've done nothing and you've got no thirst to slake but you want to drink beer. This might occur during social occasions, watching live music, football and so on, and is well suited to a quaffable, fairly neutral-tasting lager.

BEER AND FOOD

Matching beer with food is the big new trend but like most big new trends (or BNTs), if you scratch the surface a bit you discover it's been going on for years. Anyone who loves a beer has been drinking beer with food without even thinking about it. It doesn't require a PhD in the symbiosis of alpha and amino acids to know that beer and food go pretty well together. What better match is there than a cold beer and a potato crisp? Who has not enjoyed the particular pleasure in the way a quenching lager extinguishes the fire in a particularly combustible curry? To experience the exquisite gastronomical connection between a true pilsner with a homemade pretzel covered in rock salt, is one of the all-time mortal pleasures. I'm not going to go into the highly complicated and essentially boring science behind why some foods work and some don't, suffice to say that experimentation is half the fun. But just to get you started, following are some favourite and not-so-favourite beer foods.

Good beer and food matches

Meat pies; corned beef sandwiches; fish cakes; kebabs; rollmops; chips, of all sorts; nuts, of all sorts; fried seafood; fried food in general; pickled food; soft white mould cheeses; Thai food; Indian food; eggs.

Not good beer and food matches

Chocolate; fancy French cooking; soup, of all sorts; sweet food.

BUYING AND DRINKING BEER

Buying fresh

There are two things to be wary of when buying for freshness: 'use by' dates and the container the beer comes in. Obviously as far as the date goes, the fresher the better, but containers are a little more complicated. Brown glass is better for cutting out harmful UVs than green glass, while clear glass should simply be banned. If in doubt as to the freshness of a beer, go for a can over a stubby.

Buying imported

Globalisation is not a beer drinker's best friend. Whereas buying 'imported' beer once meant that you were getting something imported with all its eccentricities and exoticness intact, now in many cases you are buying the Aussie version of the recipe (with a few imported ingredients). While it makes sense from an environmental point of view – it saves shipping beer, which is mostly water, halfway around the world – it rarely makes sense from a taste point of view. Rarely does a 'brewed under licence' product taste as good, or even the same, as the original. So if you're buying imported beer and want imported beer, read the label carefully. Also be aware that in most cases, not only do you pay more for imported brews you get less beer – 330ml versus the 375ml in a standard Australian stubby.

Temperature

The ideal temperature for all the beers contained in this book is 4–6°C. Ideally 4°C for bottom lager styles and 6°C for ales, but 4–5°C is a good compromise.

Glassware

A good glass designed for the beer makes a big difference to how it tastes. Many crappy Aussie lagers wouldn't have been allowed to exist if we'd been sipping them out of pilsner glasses instead of out of the stubby or can. The way that the open mouth of a glass lets you inhale the beer as you sip, provides all sorts of olfactory goodies a slug on a stubby doesn't. Generally speaking, tall, slender pilsner glasses are prescribed for lager and stouter more open-mouthed glassware for ales.

HOW THE PROFILES WORK

Name:
That's pretty obvious.

Alcohol:
You can tell a lot about how a beer will taste and how many you can consume by the number on the side of the bottle. Alcohol provides texture and body, as well as being the engine that propels flavour. A standard lager is normally around 4.8% alcohol. A premium beer is up to 5.0% and a high-alcohol beer above 6.0%. Down at the other end, a light sits at around 2.5% and a mid-strength at 3.5%.

The scores:
Here's what the numbers mean:

0–50	Poisonous
51–60	Barely potable
61–70	Potable, but not recommended
71–80	Okay beer
81–90	Better beer
91–100	The best beer

The good:
Every beer has something to recommend it.

The bad:
It's very easy to be critical.

Best for:
Beer is a multi-faceted, multi-sided, malt-based beverage – some beers inspire thoughts of food, others don't; some are suited to occasions, others to particular thirsts.

Colour, condition and carbonation:
You can tell a fair bit about a car, (or anything else for that matter) by how it looks – and beer is no different. Colour gives an indication of style, and the type of malt used. Condition relates to the head and the way the beer pours, and carbonation takes into account the look of the head, the size of the bubble and the foam – or lacing – the head leaves on the sides of the glass. If everything seems in order on the aesthetic front, it's time to lift the bonnet and take a sniff.

Under the hood:
Contrary to what you might think, most of your sense of taste is in your nose, so smelling a beer is pretty important. The aroma contains a beer's identity – its charisma, its pheromones and much of the love or hate stuff about it. But for identifying the real basics – sweet, bitter, sour and so on – you've got to put it in your mouth.

Performance:
Beer is a product taken orally, not nasally, and no matter how good a beer smells, it's the performance in the mouth that ultimately counts. How does it travel? Does it stall on the mid-palate? Does it race through without touching the sides? The balance of sweetness and bitterness must be right and it must finish well. It's a balancing act that is actually quite tricky.

STANDARD

CHAPTER ONE

In many ways, standard beer is the true beer – it is the daily bread, the social lubricant, the fuel of life, and the (mostly) amber liquid that drives this country. Standard beer is quaffable, quenching and although 'a quiet one' might be suggested, it is designed to be consumed in the plural. Standard beer is the bread and butter of a beer company – and any brewery that can't brew a decent standard beer ought to give up and go home.

But brewing an ordinary beer that can be consumed one after the other without palate fatigue is not an easy thing. As in most things, the difference between subtle and downright boring is a very fine line. Any homebrewer knows that beer can develop strong, dominating flavours – malt and hops are not shy. So, the skill in the standard brew is to make a beer that doesn't actually taste too 'beery' – but does actually taste like something.

Here is where we find where that dreaded 'A' word mentioned earlier (page 18) comes into play. A word that brewers use in hushed tones and don't like mentioned beyond the confines of the brewery tearoom. The word is 'adjunct' – it's not really a swearword until you apply it to beer. Adjuncts have had a bad rap, but they aren't all bad – without them, the sessional standard brews we know and love would not exist. The problem is that it doesn't sound nearly as good for a lager to brag that it is 'brewed with the purest water, the freshest hops – and the finest cane sugar'. So the sugar, rice and corn that go into our everyday beers rarely appear on their labels.

It's the clever manipulation of ingredients, including adjuncts, in the making of their mainstream beers that gives the major breweries their house style. It's their distinguishing mark and it rarely changes. The head winemaker at one of Australia's largest wine companies once told me that when they tried to improve the style and quality in one of their best-selling cask reds, they were besieged by irate consumers. Familiarity for most consumers is more important than quality. Consistency is critical in everything from Vegemite to Weet-Bix to cask wine, but when it comes to standard-grade beer – it is crucial.

Many Australians have now got the flavour profile of VB, XXXX or Tooheys so deeply etched in their DNA that if a brewery were to change the recipe they'd risk a riot. So, if you don't really like the taste of VB, XXXX or Tooheys, don't wait for the beer to change – because it won't. Get yourself another brew. There are plenty to choose from in this chapter.

BOAG'S DRAUGHT

Well made, flavoursome standard brew. If quality were a criteria it would be consumed Australia-wide in the place of other mainstream products.

Alcohol: 4.7%

The good:
Quaffability, good ingredients and identifiable style.

The bad:
It's not as renowned as it should be.

Best for:
Sessions, quenching – it's a good all-rounder.

Colour, condition & carbonation:
Yellow gold, first-class head retention and sticky lacing. It looks the goods.

Under the hood:
There's a fair bit of what smells like Pride of Ringwood hops, which puts it in the Aussie lager olfactory zone. But there's something fresh about it compared to other products.

Performance:
Like a good story, this beer has a proper beginning, middle and end. A good balancing act.

SCORE: 89

BOAG'S ST GEORGE

A girlie beer designed for a market that doesn't really like the taste of proper beer – this one is way out of balance.

Alcohol: 4.8%

The good:
It's Tasmanian.

The bad:
The big ones – balance, aroma and taste.

Best for:
Using in your beer batter.

Colour, condition & carbonation:
Yellowy-gold in colour with effervescent carbonation.

Under the hood:
This beer has a sweet aroma that recalls cheap sweet wine.

Performance:
A lick of sweet fizziness and then nothing. Back to the drawing board for the folk at Boag's.

SCORE: 70

BUDWEISER

The epitome of adjunct beer – looks like beer, feels like beer, but has hardly any taste at all!

Alcohol: 4.9%

The good:
The label is iconic.

The bad:
It calls itself the King of Beers, which is a little like Kraft processed cheddar being the King of Cheeses.

Best for:
Those who don't really like the taste of beer.

Colour, condition & carbonation:
It looks the goods – nice head, pale yellow gold with good bubble.

Under the hood:
An olfactory search does reveal a little honeyed malt and some green hop characters – but you really have to look.

Performance:
This beer is like a clean, well-mannered guest that doesn't offend but doesn't leave an impression either. The finish is not wanting, it's just empty – except for a distant detergent-like note.

SCORE: 80

CARLTON COLD

This is one strangely successful beer – given its flavour and taste.

Alcohol: 4.6%

The good:
It's cold and wet.

The bad:
The label claims that it is specially brewed to stay fresher for longer – yet it's in a clear bottle, which means it goes stale faster.

Best for:
Drinking when there's nothing else on the menu.

Colour, condition & carbonation:
Delicate amber colour, good lacing and carbonation.

Under the hood:
The telltale Carlton aroma here is a little less sweet than sour. There's not much malt to speak of, but there's a hint of gunpowder.

Performance:
This is a beer that seems to want to sit at the front of the mouth and not much at the back. It's also more sour than bitter. It's a stingy beer that doesn't give much back.

SCORE: 70

CARLTON DRAUGHT

Has a taste and smell that after a hundred schooners, stubbies or pots becomes firmly lodged in the olfactory memory.

Alcohol: 4.6%

The good:
This beer is like Vegemite – distinctly flavoured with a taste that never changes from jar to jar.

The bad:
It's not draught. Those famous Carlton Clydesdales are there to subliminally tie draught horses to this so-called 'draught' beer – which actually comes out of a bottle.

Best for:
Boozing in pubs.

Colour, condition & carbonation:
The colour is pure Aussie lager, the bubbles are reasonably large and the head good.

Under the hood:
There's that classic Carlton bittersweet aroma that recalls steamed bok choy with oyster sauce.

Performance:
There's a flavour as the beer passes through the mouth that hints at chicken salt or at least chicken-flavoured crisps, otherwise the beer is easy to drink and goes down without much of a fight.

SCORE: 78

CARLTON DRY

A fairly neutral-tasting beer designed for slamming down.

Alcohol: 4.5%

The good:
Drinkable in vast quantities.

The bad:
A bit boring.

Best for:
Chilling to near freezing point to stave off the effects of heat waves.

Colour, condition & carbonation:
Fluffy head, golden colour and energetic bubble.

Under the hood:
Gentle hopping, with a faint whiff of raw nuts.

Performance:
There's a very fluffy feel to the carbonation in this beer — it slips down easily without making too much noise and finishes clean.

SCORE: 80

CASCADE DRAUGHT

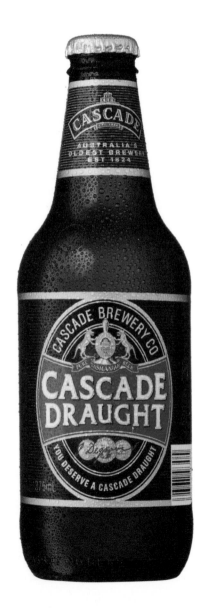

Tasmanians from the south of the state grow up on this stuff – and they're very lucky.

Alcohol: 4.7%

The good:
A standard Aussie lager that smells and tastes a little bit premium.

The bad:
It's hard to find outside of Tassie.

Best for:
Drinking on holidays in Tassie (or wherever you can get it).

Colour, condition & carbonation:
All the boxes get a big tick: head, good; bubble, spot on; colour, attractive.

Under the hood:
This is where this beer really gives a surprise. There is exotic hopping with herbal, pilsner-like, aromas and sweet malt.

Performance:
Balance and finish are the keys here. The beer slips down an absolute treat and leaves just the right amount of memory of its passing lingering on the palate.

SCORE: 90

CASCADE PALE ALE

An unusual beer for a big company. It's slightly funky and has interest and complexity – a national treasure.

Alcohol: 5.0%

The good:
Versatility – this beer can be sniffed and savoured, or slammed down on a hot day.

The bad:
It's not compulsory to have it on tap in every hotel.

Best for:
Sessioning.

Colour, condition & carbonation:
Bright gold with lacy head.

Under the hood:
There's a host of standard beer aromas as well as exotica such as Perkins Paste (in a nice way) and the fruity smell of fermenting wine.

Performance:
This beer has drive. It seems to get halfway across your palate and then make a bolt for the back of your throat – which is a good thing. It finishes with quenching lemony hops.

SCORE: 92

COOPERS ORIGINAL PALE ALE

This beer is like having a unique, slightly quirky, friend from Adelaide you can rely on in those times of thirst or need.

Alcohol: 4.5%

The good:
Original brew with the quench of a lager and the satisfaction of an ale.

The bad:
There is no bad except when the bottle shop or bar doesn't stock it.

Best for:
Pretty much everything – knocking back a couple, quenching after exertion and even to help wash down fish and chips.

Colour, condition & carbonation:
Golden blonde in colour, with a little of the infamous Cooper's cloudiness. Carbonation and lacing are both good.

Under the hood:
Herbal, lucerne-like hops meet rich malt in the most attractive way. The balance of the two is seamless and satisfying.

Performance:
Glides over the palate with just the right amount of carbonation – no clangy hops or gluey malt. For general all-purpose, four seasons beer drinking, it's hard to beat.

SCORE: 92

COOPERS SPARKLING ALE

Mainstream funky ale in a sea of lager. Iconic, individual brew, this is the EH Holden of beers.

Alcohol: 5.8%

The good:
Unique, consistent, flavoursome and different.

The bad:
Too many Coopers reds can make you go slightly berko.

Best for:
Fish and chips.

Colour, condition & carbonation:
Gold with a hint of brown and that notorious cloudiness; excellent carbonation and lacing.

Under the hood:
Large dollops of malt blend with steely hops in a wholesome way – there's a hint of Vegemite and some fruitiness too.

Performance:
Mouth filling and satisfying, this is a beer that doesn't muck around with small talk. Although quite full of body, the edges are well defined – this is a classic.

SCORE: 92

CORONA EXTRA

Quaffable, eternally trendy Mexican beer that actually does its job quite well.

Alcohol: 4.6%

The good:
Quaffing – which is why it's in this chapter.

The bad:
It should be a standard price. There's nothing particularly 'premium' about it – apart from the marketing.

Best for:
Chilling down hard and drinking by the six-pack on stinking hot days.

Colour, condition & carbonation:
Very pale gold with good bubble and bead.

Under the hood:
Nothing really outstanding in the aroma, it smells like beer in an understated way – hints of honey, corn and lemon and a tiny bit of metallic hopping.

Performance:
It zips across the palate easily and without leaving too many exhaust fumes. Balance and bittering is good. This beer is what it is.

SCORE: 86

EMU BITTER

One of the best of the WA standard brews with good hopping and excellent quenchability.

Alcohol: 4.5%

The good:
For a mainstream brew the hopping is generous and for a beer called a 'bitter' – it actually is.

The bad:
It's almost impossible to get in the eastern states.

Best for:
Steaming WA summers.

Colour, condition & carbonation:
Glowing yellow gold and not over-carbonated.

Under the hood:
There's a low-tide estuary aroma that is quite attractive. Behind that are hoppy aromas that recall weathered galvanised iron as the first raindrops hit.

Performance:
Powered by generous hopping, this brew nips across the palate with speed and grace taking the corners well and leaving a tangy bitter aftertaste.

SCORE: 89

EMU EXPORT

This is meant to be one of the best beers from the Emu 'aviary' – however, Emu Bitter is a much better beer.

Alcohol: 4.5%

The good:
It's different.

The bad:
Whoofy, swampy aromatics.

Best for:
Not much more than Western Australian beer tourism.

Colour, condition & carbonation:
Classic golden colour and quickly subsiding head.

Under the hood:
A range of rather unpleasant aromas that suggest dirty ashtrays, egg sandwiches and rusted steel.

Performance:
The balance isn't too bad, the hops are steely but it lacks drive and finish – and the beer seems to sit just above the epiglottis awaiting the next sip.

SCORE: 80

HUNTER DRAUGHT

A basic, no-frills lager designed and brewed for consuming in quantity.

Alcohol: 4.5%

The good:
Drinkable in large volumes.

The bad:
If you're looking for a funky, interesting boutique brew – this ain't it.

Best for:
Drinking instead of VB, Tooheys or other mainstream brews.

Colour, condition & carbonation:
Authentic Aussie lager colour, good lacing and carbonation.

Under the hood:
Steely, tangy hops with a real Aussie lager signature and a dollop of malt.

Performance:
A tangy steely-sided brew that, consumed ice cold, performs the job that a sessionable Australian lager should.

SCORE: 86

MELBOURNE BITTER

This is a 'point of difference' beer. If everyone's driving Tooheys and VB, Melbourne Bitter is something else – a Valiant perhaps?

Alcohol: 4.6%

The good:
A little like Valiants used to be – not particularly well engineered but recognisable.

The bad:
Maybe they should update it a bit.

Best for:
1970s-style beer drinking.

Colour, condition & carbonation:
A little darker gold than standard Aussie lager with good head and bubbles.

Under the hood:
The classic CUB sweet and sour/chow mein/bok choy aroma, with whiffs of new rubber thongs.

Performance:
There's a dollop of malt sweetness on the mid-palate and the lingering steely hops. Not badly balanced and unique in style.

SCORE: 85

RESCHS DINNER ALE

An iconic and much maligned beer which begs the question: Exactly what is a 'dinner ale', or perhaps more importantly, what isn't?

Alcohol: 4.4%

The good:
The big 800ml bottle is handy and the beer is reasonably inoffensive in an Aussie, CUB sort of way.

The bad:
For such an original concept as a 'dinner ale', the beer doesn't quite measure up.

Best for:
Not so much dinner, more for belting a few down.

Colour, condition & carbonation:
A shade darker than standard Aussie lagers, with sudsy head and less carbonation.

Under the hood:
Steely, celery-top hops with a hint of fruitiness.

Performance:
Easy to throw down, there's a slightly sweet mid-palate and mild bittering. It won't put up much of a fight against your dinner.

SCORE: 80

RESCHS ORIGINAL PILSENER

A slight return to form for the old silver bullet. It's not nearly as bad as it used to be.

Alcohol: 4.4%

The good:
Nice hopping and easy to chuck down on a hot day.

The bad:
It's not really a pilsner – it's 100% Aussie lager.

Best for:
No-frills beer drinking.

Colour, condition & carbonation:
Classic golden Aussie lager colour, with good-looking head.

Under the hood:
There are whiffs of Pride of Ringwood hops and piles of hay with sunshine on them.

Performance:
It starts strongly with the hops grabbing the sides of the mouth, but then fades a bit from that point and finishes a tad soapy.

SCORE: 83

RESCHS REAL BITTER

A fairly lonely beer on the Australian market. I'm yet to find someone to stick up for it – I certainly wouldn't.

Alcohol: 4.0%

The good:
It can be bought on special very cheaply.

The bad:
Balance, flavour, aftertaste – need I go on?

Best for:
Giving to unloved guests who don't know anything about beer.

Colour, condition & carbonation:
It has a dark colour for a lager with big bubbles and quickly subsiding head.

Under the hood:
A faintly meaty, sweaty, chemical aroma greets an inquisitive nose. There's a hint of honeyish malt underneath.

Performance:
This beer seems to travel down the centre of a drinker's mouth without venturing to the sides – and finishes without any great definition. It's not offensive, but certainly not exciting.

SCORE: 68

SHANGHAI BEER

Fairly bland lager style from China which doesn't really offer much at all.

Alcohol: 4.7%

The good:
It has a nice label.

The bad:
It's boring – barely any malt and not much hopping.

Best for:
Leaving on the shelf to admire the label. If you're looking for a Chinese beer, choose Tsingtao instead.

Colour, condition & carbonation:
Very pale gold with bubbles that sound like Alka-Seltzer.

Under the hood:
There's whiffs of cooked rice, a little honey and some faint metallic-hop aromas.

Performance:
The balance isn't bad but there's just not much to it. For a slammable, easy drinking beer, Corona is a better choice.

SCORE: 79

SOUTHWARK BITTER

South Australian brew which has a bipolar personality – a label that suggests a bitter and a taste that is something else.

Alcohol: 4.5%

The good:
Drunk on tap *in situ* in SA and really cold, it can be quite drinkable.

The bad:
A bit confused style-wise.

Best for:
Drinking in SA pubs.

Colour, condition & carbonation:
Racially pure Aussie beer colour with good head and lacing.

Under the hood:
Some quasi-Germanic hop action that hints at greenery and pilsner styles is contradicted with rather cruder bittering hops.

Performance:
Light and fluffy on the palate, it goes down easily and balance isn't bad either.

SCORE: 84

SWAN DRAUGHT

Knockback-able West Australian that is almost too easy to consume in vast quantities.

Alcohol: 4.5%

The good:
Almost goes down without you noticing.

The bad:
If you want flavour in your beer, look elsewhere.

Best for:
Big sessions.

Colour, condition & carbonation:
Pale yellowy-gold in colour with good lacing and spot-on carbonation.

Under the hood:
Tangy, steely hops promise good things.

Performance:
The hops are there but the beer seems to lack malt richness (and is probably meant to). It's a thin drink that comes into its own when consumed in volume.

SCORE: 81

TOOHEYS EXTRA DRY

An early pioneer of 'dry', which has become a favourite among certain clans and cliques.

Alcohol: 5.0%

The good:
It doesn't ruffle any feathers.

The bad:
None – unless you like your beer to taste like something.

Best for:
Drinking in quantity.

Colour, condition & carbonation:
Golden colour, good bubble with nice head.

Under the hood:
Subtle hopping with no sharp or unusual aromas.

Performance:
This is one very polite beer – it enters and leaves the mouth almost without you noticing.

SCORE: 81

TOOHEYS NEW

A classic, well-balanced mainstream brew. Not particularly exciting or bursting with charisma – but that's probably not the aim.

Alcohol: 4.6%

The good:
Easy to knock back, consistent and drinkable.

The bad:
Aficionados will look for a little more character.

Best for:
Unthinking drinking.

Colour, condition & carbonation:
A classic Aussie lager colour with better head than some of its competitors, excellent lacing and the right carbonation for the style.

Under the hood:
Gentle grassy/steely hops sit above a hint of malt.

Performance:
On the palate the beer begins and ends easily with a dollop of sweetness in the middle and a gentle finish.

SCORE: 86

TOOHEYS PILS

The name might suggest a familial resemblance to the pilsners of the Czech Republic – but the taste suggests that link is tenuous.

Alcohol: 5.2%

The good:
It's relatively drinkable.

The bad:
Contains Saaz hops – but they're a bit light on.

Best for:
Drinking when there's not much else to choose from.

Colour, condition & carbonation:
Big bubbles, sudsy head – and the lacing isn't real flash either.

Under the hood:
There is the slightest hint of Saaz but also some steely vegetal aromas that obscure the breeding and nobility of the Saaz.

Performance:
This beer is rich without being fulfilling. It doesn't quench and a little more bittering wouldn't go astray.

SCORE: 75

TOOHEYS RED BITTER

A budget, no-frills beer that in times of privation can provide sustenance.

Alcohol: 4.0%

The good:
It's cheap.

The bad:
It's not particularly satisfying.

Best for:
Drinking on a budget.

Colour, condition & carbonation:
A copper gold colour with good head and carbonation.

Under the hood:
Generic Pride of Ringwood-ish hopping meets a bit of malt – nice but not particularly exciting.

Performance:
It all performs quite well. Does its job without excelling at anything particular or being thrilling in its performance.

SCORE: 77

VICTORIA BITTER

A taste that recalls pubs, bands, bar towels and cigarette smoke.

Alcohol: 4.9%

The good:
For a hugely mainstream beer, it does have a recognisable personality.

The bad:
Finishes a bit empty.

Best for:
Basic beer drinking.

Colour, condition & carbonation:
Requisite golden amber in colour with good head retention and carbonation — there's nothing to complain about here.

Under the hood:
The CUB sweet and sour hopping is here once again, slightly vegetal with a faint hint of rusting car bodies.

Performance:
This beer excels at the entry. Hits the front palate with energy but then fades towards the finish.

SCORE: 85

WEST END DRAUGHT

Easy drinking South Australian that doesn't place too many demands on the drinker.

Alcohol: 4.5%

The good:
It's easy to put away.

The bad:
There's a slight pong to it which you either love or hate.

Best for:
South Australian pub sessions.

Colour, condition & carbonation:
There are bronze hints to the amber, while head and lacing are good.

Under the hood:
There's a little bit of a pong among the sweet smelling almost honeyed malt, a hint of steeping pearl barley and surfboard resin.

Performance:
Quite well constructed as a sessional beer, it goes down the hatch without fuss and is generally well balanced if a tad short.

SCORE: 85

WEST END EXPORT BITTER

A bit unbalanced and not particularly attractive – this lager is certainly not one of South Australia's greatest exports.

Alcohol: 4.4%

The good:
It's beer.

The bad:
Lots – flavour, balance, aftertaste.

Best for:
Drinking in South Australian pubs when the Coopers runs out.

Colour, condition & carbonation:
Authentic Aussie lager – no complaints about the looks.

Under the hood:
The nose isn't that bad – malt and clangy hops seem reasonably well placed.

Performance:
This is where the wheels fall off. The bitterness is disjointed and the beer is short and angular – and has the effect on the drinker of something that is asymmetrical but isn't meant to be.

SCORE: 77

XXXX BITTER

Easy drinking, relatively bland lager, that with good refrigeration slips down without much fuss.

Alcohol: 4.8%

The good:
It's drinkable.

The bad:
It's pretty boring.

Best for:
Loyal Queenslanders.

Colour, condition & carbonation:
Light gold, with sudsy head and very good carbonation.

Under the hood:
There's a fairly unique, if understated, hopping character overlaying a little sweet malt.

Performance:
A totally sessional brew – it slips in and down very easily, leaving barely any lingering memory of its character in its wake. Balance and carbonation are good.

SCORE: 79

XXXX DRAUGHT

Quite drinkable lager that's easy to consume cold and unthinkingly.

Alcohol: 4.5%

The good:
It brings back memories of Queensland pubs.

The bad:
Some of those memories might have been much better forgotten.

Best for:
Hot weather consumption.

Colour, condition & carbonation:
A little bronze or copper tinge to the standard yellowy-gold. Gets extra points for lacing and carbonation, which is perfect.

Under the hood:
Those signature XXXX aromas of raw peanuts and rusty pocket knives comes to the fore — you either love it or hate it.

Performance:
The balance of the beer is good, with just enough richness and plenty of hop bitterness.

SCORE: 82

PREMIUM

CHAPTER TWO

In many ways, the whole concept of 'premium' beer is abhorrent. If anything in this world should be egalitarian, it's beer. Besides, it begs the question: if a brewery isn't offering its best, what is it selling us?

Sadly, we still live in a world of hierarchies and product pyramids. The cruel truth is that the people with the most money can buy the better products. This is true of most things – a BMW is doubtless better than a Daewoo. But wait, before you revolt against the unfairness of it all, there is good news – the beer world is not entirely set up for the rich and idle. Premium beer isn't always better – some are even worse than standard brews. Premium beers exist for those with bulging pockets and also for another purpose. To get back to the car analogy, premium beer is not your everyday utilitarian vehicle. It takes a bit more money and more willpower to plough through a six-pack of Hahn Premium, than it does the equivalent volume of Tooheys. Premium beer is a Sunday drive by comparison with a commute to work.

This whole 'premium' notion is a relatively new one. Travel back in time to a bottle shop 20 years ago and there was a range of beer that seemed to be targeted for different purposes – even if most of them tasted the same. Reschs explored the glorious notion of 'Dinner Ale' (without really succeeding), there were horrible diet beers and dark ales but the only real premium beer was Crown Lager. It was the beer that you paid a fortune for when you went to a licensed restaurant. It tasted pretty much like the rest of the CUB products – except that it came in a poncy bottle.

So where and why did this whole 'premium' thing come about? The definitive history is yet to be written, but in a nutshell this is how the story goes:

In the 1980s, Australia's shores started to be invaded. Beers called Steinlager, Stella Artois, Lowenbrau and Heineken arrived and – like fancy European cars – began to show up the deficiencies of style and performance in the local Fords, Holdens and Valiants. Australians who had lived with their heads held high, confident in the knowledge that Australia produced the best beer in the world had to face the fact that Foster's was crap. A small percentage of the beer-drinking population stuck their heads in the beer-soaked bar towel and went into denial, while others took advantage of the variety and began to experiment. From that time on, the imported and premium market has been growing and the basic brews have been stable or in decline.

'Premium' is a vague term that can apply to the price as much as the beer. Put simply, the unspoken understanding between the consumer and the brewer is that a premium beer will have better (more expensive) ingredients. It will be made mostly of proper malt, instead of sugar or starch adjuncts, be more assertively flavoured with exotic hopping and come in a poncier 330ml package, instead of the standard 375ml. Good premium beer really tastes – which means it's not quite as quaffable as the adjunctified brews. It's beer designed for that innovative notion that you can stop (and be satisfied) with one or two beers – rather than the whole slab.

AMSTEL PREMIUM LAGER

High-tech brew, which has more of its sugars fermented and lower carbohydrates. Exotic hopping but low on flavour.

Alcohol: 4.7%

The good:
It has about a third less kilojoules than standard brews.

The bad:
You might actually drink more beer looking for the flavour.

Best for:
Watching waistlines.

Colour, condition & carbonation:
Pale gold in colour with lazy bubbles.

Under the hood:
Whiffs of stylish European-style hopping emerge from the glass along with a clean bitterness.

Performance:
There's no doubt the sugars are all fermented out of this beer – you can taste it. There's little malt character and consequently not much body or bounce. It slips down dry and slightly empty – the best bit is the aroma.

SCORE: 78

BARONS LAGER

Although this one ticks the 'premium' box, it could do with a tad more bittering to make it more compatible with food and big thirsts.

Alcohol: 4.9%

The good:
It's rich and malty.

The bad:
It finishes a tad sweet.

Best for:
Winter lager consumption.

Colour, condition & carbonation:
Glowing gold colour; good carbonation with quite a frothy head.

Under the hood:
There are hints of steely hops and the telltale aristocratic waft of Saaz over some sweet malt.

Performance:
Everything goes nicely until the end – the aroma is good, the richness on the palate is tasty, but there's some bitterness lacking in the finish.

SCORE: 84

BAVARIA HOLLAND BEER

Budget-priced Dutch lager imported into Australia for the Liquorland/Vintage Cellars group.

Alcohol: 5.0%

The good:
It's cheap and slightly better than Hollandia.

The bad:
It's a buyer's own brand sort of beer.

Best for:
Being thrifty.

Colour, condition & carbonation:
Pale gold with excellent sticky lacing.

Under the hood:
Grassy, citrus foliage hops on the nose and an underlying aroma that has a hint of honeydew melon about it.

Performance:
Bittering is much better with this one compared to Hollandia. It's cleaner, fresher and better balanced. All in all it's not bad for the price.

SCORE: 85

BECK'S

Now almost as widespread as VB, it's a good introduction to Germanic beer styles.

Alcohol: 5.0%

The good:
Reliable, aromatic and refreshing, it can be consumed equally happily in singles or in quantity.

The bad:
It's not imported from Germany anymore – it's made under licence by Lion Nathan (and you can tell).

Best for:
Any occasion on which you might choose a standard Aussie lager.

Colour, condition & carbonation:
Light gold with good head and lacing. Carbonation is not quite up to the smooth creaminess of the German versions.

Under the hood:
A pleasant, pilsner-esque aroma – grassy, nutty and very enticing.

Performance:
The performance on the palate disappoints slightly. The sweetness sticks out a tad and leaves the taster wanting a little bit more hop bitterness.

SCORE: 82

BLUETONGUE PREMIUM LAGER

A relatively recent arrival on the Australian premium stage, it lacks a bit of length and largesse.

Alcohol: 4.9%

The good:
It's quite easy to knock back.

The bad:
Doesn't taste as premium as it should.

Best for:
Standard beer-drinking occasions.

Colour, condition & carbonation:
Yellow gold in colour with excellent head retention.

Under the hood:
Sweet malty honey aromas are blended with the subtle whiff of steely hops.

Performance:
It's a pleasant beer to drink but is quite short. The action happens in the first and second stanzas. The third stanza is a little wanting.

SCORE: 85

BLUETONGUE TRADITIONAL PILSENER

A strange pilsner which has the hopping of a pale ale and the attitude of a lager.

Alcohol: 4.5%

The good:
It's not standard Aussie beer.

The bad:
Despite the name, it's not really a traditional pilsner.

Best for:
Experimentation.

Colour, condition & carbonation:
Creamy, lively head that stays for ages and the colour of Capilano honey.

Under the hood:
Spicy, almost fennel-like, nutty hops dominate over the top of some runny honey aromas.

Performance:
The hopping is a big part of the performance, giving the beer definite edges and a track through the mouth. It needs it though, because the malt is quite rich. This is not a sessional brew.

SCORE: 82

BYRON BAY PREMIUM ALE

The only beer produced by Byron Bay Brewing, it's a well-made premium lager with an identifiable style.

Alcohol: 5.0%

The good:
Quite well balanced with good hopping, it's a pleasant drink.

The bad:
Some other premiums offer a bit more punch.

Best for:
Something different.

Colour, condition & carbonation:
Golden lager colour with soft carbonation.

Under the hood:
Grassy hops blend with sweet malt and cooked grain aromas. It all smells natural and premium.

Performance:
There are gaps in the bittering at the beginning of this beer and in the finish that make it seem faintly dissatisfying and detract from the performance.

SCORE: 87

CARLSBERG

Soft, easy drinking lager that, despite its Danish look, is actually brewed in Malaysia under licence.

Alcohol: 5.0%

The good:
Easy drinkability.

The bad:
Not as good as the Carlsberg you get in Europe.

Best for:
Quaffing premiums.

Colour, condition & carbonation:
Carbonation is excitable, colour is pale gold.

Under the hood:
There's a nutty, paspalum grass aroma with a faintly salty tang.

Performance:
It's well put together but lacks the class and flavour of the real (Danish) thing.

SCORE: 85

CARLSBERG ELEPHANT BEER

High-alcohol lager named not after its potency, but because of the elephant gates that enclose the famous Danish brewery.

Alcohol: 7.2%

The good:
An elephant of a lager.

The bad:
It's hard to find an occasion for drinking it.

Best for:
Gentle inebriation.

Colour, condition & carbonation:
Golden amber, with a quickly subsiding head.

Under the hood:
Toffee, treacly, almost medicinal malt aromas dominate with some grassy herby hops in the background.

Performance:
Rich, but the alcohol is well hidden, except for a lingering after palate that is propelled by alcohol. Well balanced and well made.

SCORE: 88

CARLTON COLD ULTRA CHILL

An alcohol-charged Carlton brew aimed at those who focus on the effects of drinking beer more than the taste.

Alcohol: 6.5%

The good:
It's better than Carlton Cold.

The bad:
It's not the ideal way to ingest alcohol. If you want to get drunk, vodka is probably quicker.

Best for:
Drinking beer to get pissed.

Colour, condition & carbonation:
Attractive rose-gold colour, while the head and carbonation are a bit lazy.

Under the hood:
A little Pride of Ringwood hopping overlays a strange, almost spearmint, smell.

Performance:
The extra alcohol broadens the palate, but not to the level you might expect, and the beer slips down leaving the taster with that strange minty sensation. Is this a beer that freshens breath?

SCORE: 72

CARLTON CROWN LAGER

The first Australian premium still surviving despite very tough competition.

Alcohol: 4.9%

The good:
It never changes.

The bad:
It doesn't compare to most premiums on the market.

Best for:
Those places that still only have Crown on the drinks menu.

Colour, condition & carbonation:
Amber gold, good lacing and carbonation and a head that stays up for ages.

Under the hood:
Familial CUB hops, whiffs of gunpowder and egg sandwiches – and a bit of grass mowings too.

Performance:
It's a well-balanced beer with decent malt, well backed up by hopping – although the hops aren't particularly exotic.

SCORE: 86

CASCADE FIRST HARVEST

This vintage beer is made from fresh hop cones, rather than hop pellets, and is only released around the hop harvest in autumn.

Alcohol: 5.5%

The good:
Zesty, hoppy, captivating ale that is made more attractive through its limited seasonal availability.

The bad:
Not a beer for those who aren't fond of tangy hops.

Best for:
Sipping with preprandial salty, fishy bits.

Colour, condition & carbonation:
Flashing bronze colour, good head retention and clearly visible freshness.

Under the hood:
With an aroma fairly bursting with tangy, floral, steely hops, the slightly caramelly malt is well tucked away.

Performance:
Despite the rambunctious flavours, the balance is quite good and the beer moves through the mouth in the nicest possible way, leaving a long lingering aftertaste. It's a beer that's worth waiting for.

SCORE: 91

CASCADE PREMIUM LAGER

Rebadged and rejigged premium, which has lost 0.2% alcohol and 40ml of beer. Sneaky!

Alcohol: 5.0%

The good:
Rich, mouth-filling lager, with a good finish.

The bad:
Feeling suspicious – that being part of a monster like Foster's has compromised the beer slightly.

Best for:
Long, quiet ones.

Colour, condition & carbonation:
Nothing to disapprove of here – everything is in fine fettle, bright gold yellow and excellent sticky lacing.

Under the hood:
The aroma is interesting – extract of malt, bush honey and Cornetto cones combine with spicy, almost anise-like, hopping.

Performance:
Compared to its compatriot Boag's, this is a longer experience, and a slightly better brew. It's rich, but thins down after the mid-palate, where the hops kick in. It's a beer that lingers long.

SCORE: 90

CHANG BEER

Thailand's other beer export (apart from Singha) is a well put together European-styled lager.

Alcohol: 5.0%

The good:
It's favoursome and full of body.

The bad:
Keep an eye on those 'use by' dates.

Best for:
A change.

Colour, condition & carbonation:
Yellowy-gold colour, good head and bubble.

Under the hood:
Honeyed malt and Saaz-ish hops give this beer a classy Germanic aroma.

Performance:
With less full-on bittering than Singha, this beer has quite a bit of richness but is still nicely balanced. An easy drinking lager with a good creamy bubble.

SCORE: 88

COOPERS PREMIUM LAGER

Coopers' version of a lager is not a bad beer by any means, but it doesn't have the style or charisma of their ales.

Alcohol: 5.0%

The good:
It doesn't have pilsner pretensions and is in a different realm to other Aussie premiums.

The bad:
Some poncier hopping would have been nice.

Best for:
Drinking to be polite with your South Australian friends who love it.

Colour, condition & carbonation:
Yellow amber, the head dies relatively quickly.

Under the hood:
With basic steely hops and the whiff of unadorned malt, there seems to be little 'premium' about this brew.

Performance:
The action is all up the front of the palate and the beer dies away at the end – that makes this brew slightly more sessionable than other premiums.

SCORE: 81

DUKE EUROPEAN-STYLE PREMIUM LAGER

The weak link in the Duke arsenal, this one lacks a bit of punch.

Alcohol: 4.8%

The good:
A worthy attempt – even if it doesn't quite come off.

The bad:
A bit tame – it needs a little more piz-Saaz!

Best for:
Trying when you're in Queensland.

Colour, condition & carbonation:
Gentle carbonation and pale yellow gold in colour.

Under the hood:
Understated hops that smell slightly vinous, overlay the malt.

Performance:
Not offensive but not very exciting either. Performs adequately but the Duke Pale Ale is much better.

SCORE: 80

ESTRELLA DAMM

A distinctive beer that you'll find and enjoy in the Catalan region of Spain.

Alcohol: 4.6%

The good:
Refreshing with a real hop signature. If you've drunk any quantity of this one, the memories come flooding back.

The bad:
Make sure you watch those 'use by' dates.

Best for:
Hot afternoons with chips fried in olive oil.

Colour, condition & carbonation:
Pale gold, lightly carbonated with good lacing.

Under the hood:
It's mostly hops – metallic, cut grass – but it's still fresh and inviting.

Performance:
Again, it's more hops than malt. It's not a thick beer, but it's not bitter either – this one is dry and cutting, and a good quenching brew for the Australian climate.

SCORE: 89

GAGE ROADS PURE MALT LAGER

Distinctive, weighty lager from Western Australia, with thick dense malt and herby hops.

Alcohol: 4.7%

The good:
It definitely tastes premium.

The bad:
Can be a tad cloying.

Best for:
Sipping in long, fancy pilsner glasses.

Colour, condition & carbonation:
Amber gold, with good head and a decent rim of bubbles.

Under the hood:
There's plenty of sweet malt, a hint of rye bread and some interesting, almost minty, hop notes.

Performance:
It's quite a rich lager with plenty of girth and grunt, but the hopping is well applied.

SCORE: 88

GROLSCH PREMIUM LAGER

Widely acclaimed, immaculately balanced Dutch lager that puts its more famous compatriot, Heineken, in the shade.

Alcohol: 5.0%

The good:
Tastes really premium and has a style all its own.

The bad:
They've changed the ceramic caps to plastic on those iconic 500ml bottles.

Best for:
Premium moments.

Colour, condition & carbonation:
Pale gold with a steady head and good mousse.

Under the hood:
There's a combined aroma of malt and hops, which is uniquely Grolsch in character and smells of beer aristocracy. High green notes, with hints of fresh grass and hay sheds, underpinned by deeper honeyed malt notes.

Performance:
Like a finely tuned engine, this beer purrs. The balance of malt and bittering is perfect – this is lovely stuff.

SCORE: 92

HAHN PREMIUM

A beer that in company with Cascade Premium sets the standard for Australian premium beer.

Alcohol: 5.0%

The good:
Widely available, distinctive, obviously premium product, with plenty of flavour.

The bad:
It has just a little too much carbonation.

Best for:
Drinking one or two – but not six.

Colour, condition & carbonation:
Foamy carbonation lacing and pale yellow gold in colour.

Under the hood:
Smells premium – it uses Hersbrucker hops and the aroma is herbal, fresh, yet round, and full, due to the underlying malt.

Performance:
Nicely balanced brew, with first-class hopping that lingers long after being swallowed – although it's a tad over-carbonated.

SCORE: 90

HAHN SUPER DRY PREMIUM LAGER

More high-tech brewery tricks – full strength beer and lower carbs. A stubby of this delivers only 416kJ – a little less than three Saos.

Alcohol: 4.6%

The good:
Premium-smelling beer that isn't as fattening as some.

The bad:
Has a bit of a thin feeling mid-palate, which makes the drinker suspect they are missing out on something.

Best for:
Drinking beer and losing weight at the same time.

Colour, condition & carbonation:
Glowing pale gold with good lacing and carbonation.

Under the hood:
The brewers have gone to the expensive hop providores for this one. It smells very premium and invites the drinker to imbibe.

Performance:
All that aromatic foreplay leads the palate to expect something more satisfying – this beer powers through barely touching the sides. It's not cloying, but it's not mouth-filling either.

SCORE: 79

HEINEKEN

World-conquering Dutch lager brewed here under licence by Lion Nathan.

Alcohol: 5.0%

The good:
The flavour and aroma profile pretty much sums up what premium lager is about.

The bad:
It's 'imported' beer – brewed in Australia.

Best for:
One or two after a game of golf.

Colour, condition & carbonation:
Really pale in colour; excitable, sudsy head.

Under the hood:
Whiffs of fresh, enervating herbal hops season the treacly malt.

Performance:
It bears a familial resemblance to the Heinekens I once consumed at Amsterdam airport – but it isn't the same beer. It's a little more carbonated and has a little less lingering bitterness.

SCORE: 88

HOLLANDIA

The other budget Dutch brew made by the same people as Bavaria and imported into Australia for Liquorland/Vintage Cellars.

Alcohol: 5.0%

The good:
Cheap, with a whiff of premium imported lager.

The bad:
Could do with a bit more bittering.

Best for:
Cash-strapped beer enthusiasts.

Colour, condition & carbonation:
Honey gold in colour with a tendency to go flat pretty quickly, despite being well within the 'use by' date.

Under the hood:
There are some legitimate Noble hops on the nose along with a hint of honeyed malt.

Performance:
It's a beer that tends to be all front. At first everything seems in place, and just as the drinker is thinking – 'I've found a bargain here' – they're let down by the lack of a true finish.

SCORE: 83

JAMES BOAG'S PREMIUM LAGER

The challenger to Cascade's supremacy in the premium stakes. Boag's is now owned by Foster's mortal enemy, Lion Nathan – the fight is on.

Alcohol: 5.0%

The good:
Plenty to sniff and savour in this brew.

The bad:
It's just a tad out of balance.

Best for:
Just drinking one.

Colour, condition & carbonation:
Bright yellow gold with low carbonation (for a lager).

Under the hood:
Interesting intertwining of syrupy malt, an almost Gewürztraminer fruitiness and honey. There's clean, green, spicy, herbal hopping.

Performance:
The performance on the palate after the delights of the nose is somehow disappointing. A little low in bubble, it needs a little more nervy, bitter hop action to carry this much sweetness.

SCORE: 88

JAMES SQUIRE PILSENER

An idiosyncratic, gutsy lager with plenty of flavour of both hops and malt.

Alcohol: 5.0%

The good:
It's a really identifiable style with plenty going on flavour-wise – yet very drinkable.

The bad:
If you're a fan of boring beer, you're going to hate this one.

Best for:
Really good fish and chips.

Colour, condition & carbonation:
It's burnished golden colour suggests big flavour intentions; bubbles are steady and the head constant.

Under the hood:
Herbal, metallic hops with a hint of fresh coriander on the nose overlaying some nutty, toasted malt flavours.

Performance:
Balance is the key in this brew. The bittering hops provide book ends at the start and finish, keeping the rich palate in check.

SCORE: 92

KILKENNY IRISH ALE

Widely distributed Irish ale, which was originally a brand for export – riding on the back of the Guinness and Irish pub fads.

Alcohol: 4.3%

The good:
Has a creamy head and good bittering.

The bad:
The canned widget can cause some problems.

Best for:
Pizza – with loads of anchovies.

Colour, condition & carbonation:
Cloudy mahogany in colour, with an excellent creamy head that lasts for ages and is quite excitable on first opening.

Under the hood:
Coffee and burnt malt aromas mix with lighter, fruitier, estery ones in an inviting manner.

Performance:
The hops cut in early, outlining the ale and finishing it off. Tangy and textural, they really make their presence felt.

SCORE: 87

KIRIN

Calling itself (in olive oil parlance) 'first press beer', this Japanese lager is brewed under licence by the giant Lion Nathan.

Alcohol: 5.0%

The good:
Spicily hopped with a light, soft palate – it's well put together.

The bad:
It's not imported, it's brewed in Australia.

Best for:
A quiet one.

Colour, condition & carbonation:
Pale gold with good lacing – everything is how it should be.

Under the hood:
There's a good range of hop aromas with nice depth and plenty of freshness. However, the hopping does smell of an Aussie production.

Performance:
Balance is excellent, bittering is moderate – but at 6°C, it performs very well across the palate.

SCORE: 87

KNAPPSTEIN RESERVE LAGER

Paul Smith, the winemaker at Knappstein, has come up with this very impressive Bavarian-style brew using the New Zealand super hop, Sauvin.

Alcohol: 5.6%

The good:
This beer looks and tastes premium in every respect.

The bad:
It also sells for a very premium price.

Best for:
Sipping out of tall, expensive beer glasses with smoked trout canapés.

Colour, condition & carbonation:
Coppery gold with good head retention, it's not highly carbonated.

Under the hood:
Big whiffs of fruity, flowery Sauvin hops mix with rich malt, giving the impression of very expensive ingredients. Underneath the opening are squash balls fresh out of the box hiding among herbage.

Performance:
Plenty of power and bite here – while the malt is very mouth-filling, the bitterness kicks in early and stops everything from going flabby.

SCORE: 92

KRONENBOURG
1664

A locally brewed version of the French classic which is remarkably successful.

Alcohol: 5.0%

The good:
Identifiable – it takes you back to *demi pressions* in bars in Paris.

The bad:
It's a tad sweet.

Best for:
Nostalgia-cising about France.

Colour, condition & carbonation:
Bright rose-gold with good carbonation.

Under the hood:
Kronenbourg uses a hop grown in Alsace called Strisselspalt, which gives a unique citrusy gardenia fragrance, that is here in force.

Performance:
It's a sweet lager but matched by good bittering. This brew is best suited to a long quiet one rather than a quick six-pack.

SCORE: 87

LEFFE BLONDE

Fruity, yeasty brew with appreciable sweetness from the famous Belgian abbey brewery, Notre-Dame de Leffe.

Alcohol: 6.6%

The good:
This is a beer with a pedigree that dates back to 1240.

The bad:
It's a terrible quencher.

Best for:
Inquisitive drinking.

Colour, condition & carbonation:
Honey gold, good head and good clarity.

Under the hood:
Here's where things get a bit funky – estery aromas, banana Paddle Pops, raspberries with icing sugar and candied orange peel.

Performance:
Quite a high degree of sweetness, richness (check out the alcohol content) and lots of fruitiness, which narrows down with some bitterness. It does cloy a little though.

SCORE: 86

LITTLE CREATURES PILSNER

This beer is about as pale as lager gets. While it's subtly flavoured compared to most Little Creatures brews, the balance and persistence are very good.

Alcohol: 4.6%

The good:
Fine balance, good flavour and excellent carbonation.

The bad:
Not jumping out of the glass screaming 'Saaz!', like some pilsners.

Best for:
Stylish quenching after a set or two of tennis.

Colour, condition & carbonation:
Pale, almost lemony, colour, with foamy carbonation and nice lacing.

Under the hood:
Smells premium – nutty aromas, Noble hops and good balance.

Performance:
This one has an easy, sophisticated drinkability. It's very sessionable, with subtlety and balance being strong points.

SCORE: 90

LÖWENBRÄU ORIGINAL

Löwenbräu is a little like BMW motorcycles – the machinery is good and the ride is smooth, but there are more exciting trips.

Alcohol: 5.2%

The good:
Dependable Bavarian beer with wide distribution.

The bad:
It isn't the greatest quencher, and is best consumed in the cooler months.

Best for:
Australian Octoberfests.

Colour, condition & carbonation:
Light gold in colour, the head is relatively sudsy and dies fairly quickly.

Under the hood:
Very polished and appealing aroma at once smelling of warmed honey and sunshine on fresh hay and at the same time wet, mild steel.

Performance:
This is a beer that carries a bit of malt and likes to sit on the mid- to back-palate. The finish dies a little towards the end.

SCORE: 85

MATILDA BAY BOHEMIAN PILSNER

A prince of pilsners — it smells and tastes like pilsner and doesn't use that hallowed word in vain.

Alcohol: 4.7%

The good:
A first-class, proper-tasting pilsner produced in Australia.

The bad:
It can be hard to get.

Best for:
Measuring how far below the mark some other things called 'pilsner' really are.

Colour, condition & carbonation:
Rose-gold in colour with good fluffy head retention and bright clarity.

Under the hood:
Luxurious cool, herbal cleanliness of Saaz hops exudes from the glass, along with some serious malt.

Performance:
While there's plenty of flavour and power to this Aussie pilsner, the level of bittering hops is just right — inviting another sip, another swallow and, almost certainly, another stubby.

SCORE: 93

MILLER GENUINE DRAFT

Easy-drinking, cleverly made lager that is wholly and solely designed for unthinking drinking.

Alcohol: 4.7%

The good:
It's easy to knock back.

The bad:
It's almost too easy to knock back.

Best for:
Americana-themed parties.

Colour, condition & carbonation:
Pale gold, excellent lacing and freshness.

Under the hood:
Faint aroma of roast corn mixed with candied honey and some gentle hopping.

Performance:
Flits across the palate and barely touches down. A hint of honeyed richness appears before disappearing – beer like this one can be consumed in number without really noticing.

SCORE: 85

MOOSEHEAD LAGER

A tasty Canadian take on the standard lager recipe, with unique, clean hopping and big flavours.

Alcohol: 5.0%

The good:
Easily recognisable and not shy.

The bad:
Beware of stale samples.

Best for:
Experimentation.

Colour, condition & carbonation:
Pale gold with a bronze tinge, good mousse (no pun intended) and head retention.

Under the hood:
There's plenty of hoppy activity for a mass-market lager – the hops have a green, almost minty fresh, aroma and sit over the top of treacly malt.

Performance:
The effect of this rich lager is refreshing – from the zesty aroma, to the bittering, which has a herbal zing to it.

SCORE: 89

PERONI NASTRO AZZURRO

A lager without the cache (or marketing) of the world famous Heinekens et al., but this one can easily stand up to the best.

Alcohol: 5.1%

The good:
It's got its own style – big, malty, but seasoned with plenty of herby hops.

The bad:
Hard to consume by the six-pack.

Best for:
Long, cold, slow ones.

Colour, condition & carbonation:
Pale with excellent lacing and a steady head.

Under the hood:
Aristocratic hops waft from the glass, with equally abundant aromas of rich malt.

Performance:
It's a rich lager but encased in judiciously applied fresh, aromatic and bittering hops. The effect is balanced and very pleasant and ultimately satisfying – 330ml goes a long way.

SCORE: 92

PILSNER URQUELL

Iconic brew from the lager holy land of Pilsen in the Czech Republic, which, despite fame and globalisation, still tastes exotic.

Alcohol: 4.4%

The good:
Intensely hoppy, richly malty and truly delicious lager.

The bad:
It can suffer from a lack of freshness. Choose a shop with a high Urquell turnover.

Best for:
Smoked salmon.

Colour, condition & carbonation:
Bronze and darker than standard lager, the head retention isn't too flash but carbonation is good.

Under the hood:
An aroma which should serve as a model for premium lagers – it's spicy, grassy and seasons the treacly malt in a most attractive way.

Performance:
This is not shy beer – the big malty tastes are countered with very good bittering, leaving the impression that you have really experienced something. This is not a quaffer – it's a sipper.

SCORE: 95

RED ANGUS PILSENER

Brewed at De Bortoli in Griffith, this is a rich lager that, despite the name, isn't quite a pilsner.

Alcohol: 4.8%

The good:
It's not short on flavour or richness.

The bad:
It's a bit unbalanced, needing more aromatic hops.

Best for:
Slow sipping.

Colour, condition & carbonation:
Golden yellow, with a steady loosely packed head and good lacing.

Under the hood:
Malt aromas abound, even leaning towards caramel, while the hops are kept well to the background.

Performance:
Malty and chunky, the hops kick in at the end but there's not enough at the beginning and middle to counter that gluey malt. This is not a well-balanced pilsner.

SCORE: 83

REDBACK CRISTAL WHEAT BEER

This is a more perfumed, lager style of wheat beer — and a halfway point between standard and wheat brews.

Alcohol: 4.5%

The good:
It really is a cleverly brewed concoction.

The bad:
The see-through bottle means that this is a beer that has to be drunk fresh and — like an albino — should never see the sunlight.

Best for:
Dips and rice crackers.

Colour, condition & carbonation:
Glowing yellow gold, the head sinks faster than the original Redback but holds its carbonation well.

Under the hood:
There's an interesting mixture of grassy hops, rusty cars, a hint of yeast lees and a refreshing citric bite.

Performance:
There's more length to this brew compared to the original — due, no doubt, to the lager yeast and slower fermentation; it's a longer experience.

SCORE: 89

REDBACK ORIGINAL WHEAT BEER

Australia's first wheat beer is now over 20 years old and is wheat beer's answer to VB – at least in terms of distribution.

Alcohol: 4.7%

The good:
Refreshing, sessionable and nicely balanced.

The bad:
Like most wheat beers there's less palate weight than standard brews, but that's not a fault – just a point of difference.

Best for:
Sinking a couple on a really hot day with freshly shucked Pacific oysters.

Colour, condition & carbonation:
Honey gold, with good head and steady bubbles.

Under the hood:
Honey and lemon zest mixed with cold steel, cooked pearl barley, a hint of wet carpet and old oranges. It's all nicely integrated.

Performance:
Wheat beers don't lie around on your palate in the same way as barley-based brews. That makes them seem a little short, but adds to their refreshing quality. The balance is well done.

SCORE: 90

SMB BULLOCKS PILSNER

An authentic pilsner style – as far as ingredients are concerned – that offers a bit of a different take on the recipe.

Alcohol: 4.5%

The good:
Tasty quality beer from a good local mini-brewery.

The bad:
The hopping balance could be adjusted slightly.

Best for:
Drinking après ski.

Colour, condition & carbonation:
Golden colour, good carbonation, mousse and lacing.

Under the hood:
The aroma recalls quality European pilsners with that grassy, nutty, hay shed, granary aroma.

Performance:
The flow of this brew through the mouth and the balance of sweetness to bitterness is where the main fault lies – it all seems to lean towards the front of the mouth and the finish is slightly empty.

SCORE: 86

SOL

A belt-it-back lager in the Corona mould – albeit a little more rustic and unpolished in style.

Alcohol: 4.5%

The good:
Tastes exactly like the sort of beer you'd get in a daggy Mexican café.

The bad:
It doesn't really stand up to international lager competition – and certainly isn't premium.

Best for:
Surfing holidays in Baja.

Colour, condition & carbonation:
Pale gold in colour with low carbonation and a head with a tendency to die.

Under the hood:
There are nuances of metallic hops with a hint of pong and not much in the way of malt.

Performance:
This beer is not meant to be savoured. Belt it down as cold as possible and it does the trick. There's not much to it and it doesn't offend.

SCORE: 82

SOUTHWARK PREMIUM LAGER

A strange beer. While tasting premium, it seems a bit wrong – a bit like a 'thongs and shorts' bloke in a tuxedo.

Alcohol: 5.0%

The good:
It's unique.

The bad:
It's not at all refreshing.

Best for:
Loyal Southwark-drinking South Australians.

Colour, condition & carbonation:
Nothing wrong here – bright golden yellow in colour with a good head.

Under the hood:
Big whiffs of malt smelling of bush honey, blends with some European hop action, but it all seems a little out of whack.

Performance:
It's a thick beer that lies on the tongue and while it tastes full of premium ingredients, you find yourself wishing for a little less.

SCORE: 83

STAROPRAMEN

This difficult-to-pronounce lager from Prague doesn't measure up to the standard set by its fellow-countryman, Pilsner Urquell.

Alcohol: 5.0%

The good:
It has a malty style with good bitterness.

The bad:
It doesn't taste too fresh.

Best for:
Fried whitebait.

Colour, condition & carbonation:
Quite bronze with bad head retention and a tendency to go flat.

Under the hood:
Spicy, nutty hops overlay caramelly malt.

Performance:
The performance on the palate disappoints – the beer is very malty and the hopping isn't powerful enough to balance it.

SCORE: 81

STEINLAGER

A beer that set the premium beer market on fire in the early '90s — and still tastes the goods.

Alcohol: 5.0%

The good:
This beer uses Green Bullet hops, which gives Steinlager a taste profile a bit different to its peers.

The bad:
It doesn't have the richness of some of its competitors, but in some contexts that's a good thing

Best for:
Alfresco stubby consumption.

Colour, condition & carbonation:
Pale in colour, with excellent lacing and carbonation.

Under the hood:
Grassy, fresh hay bales and sacks of grain — it's a fresh, invigorating aroma. The hopping is excellent and for a premium beer it's a pleasant change not to smell the ubiquitous Noble varieties.

Performance:
Invigorating on the palate. While not as rich and palate-coating as some premiums, it is a better choice for hot weather consumption.

SCORE: 88

STELLA ARTOIS

Have you noticed a difference in Stella? It's now brewed under licence in Australia by CUB. It's fresher than the imported stuff but not as good.

Alcohol: 5.2%

The good:
It's a widely available premium and a 'green' imported beer – because it's made locally, it doesn't have the food miles of the Belgian stuff.

The bad:
The locally made Stella is not a patch on the real deal.

Best for:
Stylish stubby consumption.

Colour, condition & carbonation:
Pale yellow gold with good carbonation and lacing.

Under the hood:
The sweet malt is the dominant aroma underpinned by some gentle hops.

Performance:
The beer is nicely balanced, frothy, and travels through the mouth without lumps and bumps, but could do with a little more bittering on the finish.

SCORE: 85

TOOHEYS EXTRA DRY PLATINUM

A high-alcohol neutral-tasting lager designed for a market that values alcohol over flavour.

Alcohol: 6.5%

The good:
It's really easy to knock back (probably dangerously so).

The bad:
It lacks character and finishes a bit empty.

Best for:
Drinking to get pissed.

Colour, condition & carbonation:
Delicious-looking honey gold colour with fine bubbles and gentle head.

Under the hood:
The aroma is subtle – a whiff of steely hops can be found after searching and there's not much malt character due probably to a fair bit of adjunct.

Performance:
There's plenty of palate weight, thanks to the alcohol, and the beer slips down easily and finishes without any lingering nasties.

SCORE: 79

VICTORIA BITTER ORIGINAL ALE

A response by the folks at CUB to all the tasty, generous brews on the market. It begs the question – if VB used to taste like this, why did they change it?

Alcohol: 4.6%

The good:
True flavour – real malt and pleasant hopping.

The bad:
Despite its pretensions to boutique-dom, it still tastes like a CUB beer.

Best for:
Sausage sandwiches.

Colour, condition, & carbonation:
The colour is exciting – a couple of shades darker than trad VB, it's deep bronze with sticky lacing and good head retention.

Under the hood:
There's some treacly malt there, along with the peanut oil hop aromas. The brewers could have been a little more generous with the hops and there is still that identifiable bok choy CUB signature.

Performance:
It has way more palate richness than standard VB, and has good balance and a steady, if not lingering, finish.

SCORE: 88

DIESEL

CHAPTER THREE

Heavy fuel, antifreeze, liquid ball bearings – call it what you like – but when it comes to cool climate beer drinking, dark beer is a brass monkey's best friend. But oils ain't oils and lobbing all black beer in the same category is just plain wrong. The world of black beers is as diverse as that of the blondes. With a little dark malt and yeast in the tank, the road for the adventurous brewer is wide open. From stouts to porters to bocks and everything in between, there really is a black beer for every purpose.

Stout

In much the same way that people call pens 'biros' and vacuum cleaners 'hoovers', stout is pretty much thought of as Guinness, because of that world-conquering Irish concoction. However, Guinness is but one take on the genre that is stout. There are sweet stouts, dry stouts, cream stouts, invalid stouts and innumerable others. Some are delicious and fortifying – an espresso coffee, a tasty meal and a very good beer all in a single glass – while others are yucky black muck. It's a style of beer that needs to be approached with caution, conviction and a little experience.

Porter

'We sat in Grogan's with our faded overcoats finely disarrayed on easy chairs in the mullioned snug. I gave a shilling and two pennies to a civil man who brought us in return two glasses of black porter, imperial pint measure. I adjusted the glasses to the front to each of us and reflected on the solemnity of the occasion, it was my first taste of porter.'
Flann O'Brien, At Swim-Two-Birds, 1939

One's first taste of a good porter is doubtless unforgettable, but there are many beer-drinking veterans who are yet to experience the delights of this black beer. Porter is a beer style in decline. Stout is now the more famous black beer, and it evolved as a heavier version of porter – 'stout porter', as it was called. Porter is a lighter black beer and much easier to drink in quantities than stout.

Bock

Whereas most black beers are top-fermented ales, bock is a strong lager made from dark roasted malt. Traditionally, they have an alcohol content of 6%. A dopple bock (double bock) isn't actually double the alcohol – they tend to be around 7–8% alcohol.

Dark lager

As the title suggests, this is a close relation to bock and is pretty much as described – the use of dark malts with a lager-style fermentation and maturation. The best example in this book is Matilda Bay's Dogbolter.

Dark ale

This is a style of beer that has the look of a porter, but the body and palate of lighter ale. Tooheys Old is the classic Australian example.

BARONS BLACK WATTLE ORIGINAL ALE

Dark ale with plenty of caramelly malt – and with wattleseed that seamlessly adds to the flavour and aroma.

Alcohol: 5.8%

The good:
Complexity – there's heaps to sniff and savour here.

The bad:
If you don't like big, rich flavours – stay away.

Best for:
A quiet one on a cool day.

Colour, condition & carbonation:
Very attractive – red mahogany colour, active head and good lacing.

Under the hood:
Where shall I start? Some spicy, citrusy, fruity aromas and a little grassiness combine with a bit of Vegemite, dark treacle, iced coffee and even roast sweet potato – nice.

Performance:
There's generous richness and flavours that hit off receptors as it passes from orifice to oesophagus.

SCORE: 91

BEECHWORTH ROBUST PORTER

Heavily roasted dark beer, this is one of the better Beechworth brews.

Alcohol: 5.2%

The good:
Well-balanced tasty porter with big flavour.

The bad:
Not too much, this is interesting beer.

Best for:
Bitey cheddar grilled on dark rye bread.

Colour, condition & carbonation:
Scary black in colour, the lacing is good and the bubbles big.

Under the hood:
Powerful mocha and chocolate pudding aromas mix with a hint of roast pumpkin.

Performance:
Big roast flavours swarm the palate but without becoming overbearing or cloying, while the bittering hops do their job admirably.

SCORE: 85

CARLTON BLACK DARK ALE

A dark ale which isn't so flavoursome as to discourage a would-be sessioner.

Alcohol: 4.4%

The good:
Easy-drinking dark ale with nothing too disagreeable.

The bad:
Seasoned black-beer drinkers will be looking for a bit more action.

Best for:
Cool climate pub sessions.

Colour, condition & carbonation:
The colour of Bonox, it's dark brown with a slight reddish tinge, while the head fades quickly.

Under the hood:
While there's definitely some coffee/mocha characters going on, there's also an aroma of inexpensive shiraz — which may or may not be a bad thing.

Performance:
There's a fleeting chocolatey nature to the flavour that dissipates with mild bittering. This brew doesn't hang around long.

SCORE: 76

CARLTON SHEAF STOUT

A dark caramelly/chocolatey stout that is a surprisingly good brew.

Alcohol: 5.7%

The good:
Flavour – for a big company brew this stout isn't shy.

The bad:
Just a tad too sweet – a smidgeon more bittering would be good.

Best for:
Cold, rainy days.

Colour, condition & carbonation:
Liquorice coloured with the brownness staining the creamy head. This stout has good carbonation and looks the business.

Under the hood:
An estery aroma greets the olfactories that hints at Galliano. There's also a sniff of cold instant coffee and chocolate-cake mix.

Performance:
Creamy and coating, the stout spreads chocolatey, slightly burnt flavours around the mouth before quickly departing, leaving a distinct palate memory.

SCORE: 88

CASCADE STOUT

Rich, tangy stout with enticing roasted malt flavours and no shortage of grunt or power.

Alcohol: 5.8%

The good:
The coffee mocha flavours are well balanced by some bittering hops.

The bad:
The label. The bloke on the front, Fatty Appleton, was famous at Cascade for being able to carry a couple of firkins (barrels) under each arm – but his caricature doesn't make him look tough, so much as constipated.

Best for:
Cool Tasmanian-type weather.

Colour, condition & carbonation:
Sudsy, lacy, brown-tinged head, dark red-brown colour and carbonation that is on the less-vigorous side.

Under the hood:
Dark chocolate meets roasting coffee. There's a slight hint of fennel there too – all very attractive.

Performance:
Again, it's the balance that sets this one apart. The burnt impressions taper down to a pleasant finish. This is good Aussie stout.

SCORE: 87

CASTLEMAINE CARBINE STOUT

A quite well put together Queensland stout bearing the name of a famous racehorse.

Alcohol: 5.1%

The good:
Balance – and the label is pretty cool too.

The bad:
Can seem a little one-dimensional compared to some other Aussie stouts.

Best for:
Kransky and onion on a white bread roll.

Colour, condition & carbonation:
Dark mahogany with reddish-brown tints and brown tainted head.

Under the hood:
Mocha, Marmite and hints of fruity yeast.

Performance:
Not as rich as you might expect – the balance is quite good and the beer is quite lithe.

SCORE: 86

CASTLEMAINE

CARBINE

SINCE 1924

STOUT

375 mL

COOPERS BEST EXTRA STOUT

This is a cult stout – a rare beer that actually improves in the bottle. Coopers' freaks swear by it and claim it fixes all sorts of ailments.

Alcohol: 6.3%

The good:
It's not shy of hiding its goodies. What you smell is pretty much what you get here – plenty of burnt rich flavours and not too much sweetness.

The bad:
Apparently, if you drink a lot of this stuff you put on weight like a lot-fed cow.

Best for:
Cold roast beef and horseradish sandwiches.

Colour, condition & carbonation:
A brooding dark browny-black with tawny-coloured fluffy head and creamy carbonation.

Under the hood:
Oodles of aroma ranging from dark chocolate to molasses and cold espresso.

Performance:
Mocha-like flavours float across the palate quite effortlessly and it finishes with a lingering bitterness in the nicest possible way. This is high-quality stout.

SCORE: 90

GUINNESS DRAUGHT

The brand that changed black beer drinking the world over. An iconic brand and an iconic drink.

Alcohol: 4.2%

The good:
It's imported (or at least this can is) and is not made under licence by CUB.

The bad:
Even though it's way better than the stuff you used to get here, it's still not what you got in the pubs back in good old Ireland a decade ago.

Best for:
Long quiet ones.

Colour, condition & carbonation:
Black with henna highlights and dense creamy head.

Under the hood:
Roasting coffee, liquorice, cooking chocolate – a whole gamut of black aromas.

Performance:
The big difference between this and the CUB-brewed versions of the hallowed brew is bitterness. While the beer can be creamy and a bit floppy on the palate, the edginess of the bittering hops keeps it on line.

SCORE: 85

HUNTER OLD

Dark ale in the Tooheys Old mould but lacking the execution of that brew.

Alcohol: 4.5%

The good:
Different-tasting dark ale for lovers of Tooheys Old.

The bad:
The balance of flavours and textures isn't great.

Best for:
Chip butties.

Colour, condition & carbonation:
Dark mahogany with a reddish gleam, the head is sudsy and quick to dissipate.

Under the hood:
Aromas of fish oil mix with a Bonoxy, burnt coffee aroma that isn't attractive.

Performance:
There are pleasant bitter chocolate flavours and a little estery fruitiness, but the beer gets a little watery on the back palate before the sour finish kicks in — the effect is a bit disjointed.

SCORE: 77

JAMES SQUIRE PORTER

A creamy, sudsy dark beer which offers a little less weight than a standard Aussie stout.

Alcohol: 5.0%

The good:
Hopping. Dark beers can often seem a little sweet and caramelly – this one cleans up nicely.

The bad:
The froth factor is just a smidgeon too much. Be careful pouring this one.

Best for:
Hot pies on cold days.

Colour, condition & carbonation:
Bubble bath creamy head, ever so slightly tainted brown, overlays a reddy-brown liquid. The froth factor is high so the prickle of the carbonation is low.

Under the hood:
Stylish hopping and subtle roasted malts meet the nose. It's not a 'lashings of molasses' dark beer.

Performance:
Generous and creamy with a burnt edge, this porter slips down easily and leaves the palate relatively unfettered by its arrival and departure. The hopping is perfect – it's a dark beer that doesn't cloy.

SCORE: 89

MATILDA BAY DOGBOLTER DARK LAGER

A dark lager dripping in the dark flavours of chocolate, coffee and toffee – but remains surprisingly balanced.

Alcohol: 5.2%

The good:
This is a dark brew that isn't too syrupy and has impeccable balance.

The bad:
Not much – it's not particularly sessionable, but that's not the point.

Best for:
Ploughman's lunches.

Colour, condition & carbonation:
The colour of sump oil with a pillowy head that has good retention.

Under the hood:
An attractive concoction of steely, grassy hops, and toffee. Hints of lucerne hay give way to whiffs of Cornwell's Extract of Malt.

Performance:
While palate-coating and rich, the Dogbolter narrows down nicely towards the finish inviting the drinker to take another sip. Balance is the strong point.

SCORE: 91

MATILDA BAY GRAYSTON RESERVE

A unique beer for the adventurous beer drinker not afraid of the weird and wacky.

Alcohol: 6.0%

The good:
A conversation starter – this is a beer that must be talked about. Start with this interesting nugget: this is a beer that uses four types of malt and one type of hop (Hersbrucker). It's usually the other way around.

The bad:
At around $17 for a long neck, it's pretty pricey.

Best for:
Esoteric beer drinking.

Colour, condition & carbonation:
Reddish-brown in colour, with creamy head, the carbonation strikes a balance between the froth of a stout and the prickle of a lager.

Under the hood:
An exotic aroma of dried bananas, cloves and Play-Doh is countered with more traditional hopping and subtle roasted malts.

Performance:
That estery dried banana is there along with a little caramel. It's impressive in its range of flavours and coverage. An acquired taste and not a quaffer – a little bit goes a long way.

SCORE: 88

MOUNTAIN GOAT SUREFOOT STOUT

A stout with the unmistakable Mountain Goat hoof print. There's good bitterness and plenty of head.

Alcohol: 5.0%

The good:
Rich flavours, well balanced with bitter hops.

The bad:
Carbonation is a bit fluffy.

Best for:
Sipping on a cold winter's day watching your favourite code of football.

Colour, condition & carbonation:
Pouring is tricky – this is an excitable beer with loads of foam overlaying a dark, Vegemitey-coloured liquid.

Under the hood:
Unusual in a stout, the herbal, fresh hopping aromas are balanced with the roasted chocolatey ones.

Performance:
Apart from the explosive carbonation, the balance of this stout is what appeals. Richness and bitterness counteract each other very nicely.

SCORE: 89

REDOAK BELGIAN CHOCOLATE STOUT

An oatmeal stout that offers a different flavour profile to standard brews in that it has dark chocolate added to the brew.

Alcohol: 5.0%

The good:
It's unique.

The bad:
It's also an acquired taste.

Best for:
Sipping by open fires.

Colour, condition & carbonation:
Dark brown with a reddish tinge, carbonation and head are all good.

Under the hood:
This is where the fun starts. There's a blue cheese aroma overlaying the chocolatey/ coffeeish ones. There's also a whiff of melting brown sugar.

Performance:
This is a rich beer with mild carbonation, the flavours are unique and at first a little surprising, but balance and hopping is very good.

SCORE: 85

REDOAK WEE HEAVY ALE

Highly alcoholic and sweet, but well-constructed, dark ale that is not recommended for imbibing in tropical climates.

Alcohol: 8.0%

The good:
A big, tasty ale that takes no prisoners.

The bad:
Despite the sweetness and high alcohol, the balance isn't too bad.

Best for:
Sipping by a fire on a dark, stormy night.

Colour, condition & carbonation:
Vegemite-coloured with creamy spume steady head.

Under the hood:
Smells a little like a Cherry Ripe. There's also a bit of orange peel, toffee and, in the background, beef stock cubes and a hint of fish oil.

Performance:
Glides across the palate with alcohol-cushioned shock absorbers giving the impression of a very rich beer. Fortunately, the hops kick in at the end giving some finality to the proceedings.

SCORE: 88

SOUTHWARK OLD STOUT

A bit of a classic this one. In the 'A' league where alcohol is concerned – and a very good stout with food.

Alcohol: 7.4%

The good:
Style. This stout is an individual carrying its size and weight with grace and ease.

The bad:
It's hard to get and many bottle shops in this wide brown land don't stock it.

Best for:
Interesting dining experiments.

Colour, condition & carbonation:
Dark and foreboding, the chocolate-milkshake frothy head is steady and the carbonation good.

Under the hood:
There's a lot going on in this dense, dark brew – dark chocolate, liquorice and even a hint of creosote (all in the nicest possible way).

Performance:
It's amazing what a little extra alcohol can do. This stout motors across the palate, coating the mouth with flavour and departing with the lingering exhaust of bittering hops and roasted malts.

SCORE: 92

750mL

SWAN STOUT

A big stout in the Southwark tradition –
although it's not quite as good.

Alcohol: 7.4%

The good:
No shortage of flavour or
power – or alcohol.

The bad:
A smidgeon too sweet.

Best for:
A decent serve of chips
from a proper fish and chip
shop drowned in cheap,
white vinegar.

**Colour, condition
& carbonation:**
Deep mission brown with
reddish coppery tints, lasting
carbonation and head.

Under the hood:
Cocoa, Milo, marzipan and
treacle sit above a faint
tang of hops.

Performance:
This beer doesn't so much
fill your mouth as invade.
All receptors are beaten
into submission and soothed
by sweetness. The finish is
sweet/dry, but could be a
bit more of the latter.

SCORE: 87

TOOHEYS OLD BLACK ALE

Historic dark ale with subtlety as a strong suit. Not big on caramelly malt or hops, it's a good choice of brew for those new to the dark side.

Alcohol: 4.4%

The good:
Balanced and confident, it's not trying to be anything other than what it is.

The bad:
Lovers of really full-on dark beers might find it a bit short in the flavour department.

Best for:
Watching footy and eating pies.

Colour, condition & carbonation:
Reddish-brown in colour, there's an old brake fluid look to it. The head is sudsy and not particularly energetic.

Under the hood:
Complex charry aromas of roasted malt and Space Bars, and a nostalgic whiff of Drum roll-your-own tobacco blend happily with a little steely hop action.

Performance:
Flavours that hint of chocolate, nuts and pans that have roasted Japanese pumpkin, slip by before the beer disappears lightly, without any lingering nasties.

SCORE: 88

BIOFUEL

CHAPTER FOUR

Australia has been a lager lake for too long. Yes it's true that our climate is perfectly suited to the crisp, fresh flavours of bottom-fermented beer, but it's not always hot. Some places in this land experience winter and have climates perfectly suited to ale consumption. Fortunately, as the amount of beers in this chapter clearly shows, things are changing, ales are proliferating and Australia is becoming a better place to drink.

The brewers have suffered the lager lake along with the drinkers. For a brewer, it's much more fun exploring their creativity with a funky ale than beavering away at an anal lager – there's something very serious, patient and regimented about the recipe (it is German, after all). On the other hand, ale is always a work in progress. This chapter showcases the experimental, edgy, thrill-seeking side of brewing, and for those raised on a diet of VB, some of these beers might taste like they come from another planet. The trick is to keep an open mind and palate. Some of the beer styles can be confusing but most fall into just three categories – ales, pale ales and wheat beers.

Ales

Ales tend to be classed according to colour. Golden ales are almost lager-like in their drinkability; amber ales are darker with more roast malt character; brown ales are a sweeter style; and Irish red ales have fruitiness, but also considerable bitterness. Of course, there is much overlap within the ale family.

Pale ales

The pale ale genre has many evolutionary offshoots and probably needs a little explanation. It started as an English style, which was simply named because it was a paler than the average ale. Then came India Pale Ale, or IPA. These evolved during the days of the Raj when standard beer wouldn't last the trip from Britain. Ales were given an extra late gift of hops as a preservative and to help them survive the trip. Then there's the American pale ale style – the darling of the craft brewing industry. It's a style that's generally bigger all round – a super-duper IPA using American species of hops.

Wheat beers

The world of wheat beers is a weird one and includes the Belgian 'wit' (or white) beers that can have spices added to them as well as the German hefeweizen. Most are made from a blend of wheat and barley and some can have oats and other grains added too. What they share is a lighter body, usually some fruity citrus and banana flavours, and a cloudy look – except kristallweizen, which is filtered.

BAREFOOT RADLER

A new 'beer', with lemon and lime added – and aimed at a market that doesn't like beer.

Alcohol: 4.2%

The good:
Probably contains a little vitamin C.

The bad:
Sweet – it tastes a little like someone poured Solo in your Tooheys.

Best for:
Steering clear of.

Colour, condition & carbonation:
Honey yellow in colour, low head, with no visual hint of what's to come.

Under the hood:
The aroma really is reminiscent of Solo and a bland lager blended 60/40.

Performance:
Way too sweet – this is alcoholic soft drink.

SCORE: 65

BARONS EXTRA SPECIAL BITTER

A beer that will surprise and enlighten the most dedicated lager drinker. Generously hopped and full flavoured, it's ale as it should be.

Alcohol: 4.7%

The good:
A finish that lingers for days.

The bad:
None, it's really good.

Best for:
Consuming with pickled things, like octopus and onions.

Colour, condition & carbonation:
Copper-bronze brown with fantastic creamy head – first class as far as looks go.

Under the hood:
Roasted parsnip meets Vegemitey aromas with sweet malt and spicy, pithy hops.

Performance:
This brew covers the mouth with flavour, the bittering hops seek out the throat and continue the finish for aeons – this is one very satisfying experience.

SCORE: 91

BARONS LEMON MYRTLE WITBIER

Bottle-conditioned witbier given a little squeeze of lemon via the native lemon myrtle. It works.

Alcohol: 4.5%

The good:
Interesting, refreshing wheat beer.

The bad:
Not much to criticise.

Best for:
Fish eating.

Colour, condition & carbonation:
Cloudy, with fresh and lively carbonation.

Under the hood:
Spicy lemon zest aroma, which has whiffs of star jasmine as well.

Performance:
Glides quite effortlessly down the throat leaving a lemony sherbet aftertaste.

SCORE: 87

BARONS PALE ALE

A quality pale ale that isn't as full-on in the hop department as some boutique pale ales, but sits in its own zone quite comfortably.

Alcohol: 4.6%

The good:
Subtlety. Quality ingredients are put together in an attractive, not overt, way.

The bad:
If you like your pale ales reeking with hops, you'll find it lacking.

Best for:
Gentle thirsts.

Colour, condition & carbonation:
A hint of mahogany to the golden colour, excellent head and lacing and carbonation is spot on.

Under the hood:
This beer uses Hallertau and Sauvin hops – and you can tell. They're luxurious, not particularly biting, but very complementary. Green herbal aromas combine with lemon thyme, treacly malt and even a whiff of freshly washed cotton sheets.

Performance:
Good acceleration across the palate, fine balance and a pleasant lingering flavour.

SCORE: 89

BEECHWORTH AUSTRALIAN ALE

Funky, fruity golden ale that tastes like it comes from a micro-brewery.

Alcohol: 4.4%

The good:
It's different.

The bad:
The strange estery, fruity aromas won't appeal to everyone.

Best for:
Lovers of fruity ales.

Colour, condition & carbonation:
Bright gold in colour, the head collapses pretty quickly and there's little lacing.

Under the hood:
Banana ester derived aromas dominate with a little hop action underneath.

Performance:
It's a beer that isn't integrated – and is a bit clunky in its gear changes as it moves across the palate.

SCORE: 78

BEECHWORTH BAVARIAN WHEAT

A funky wheat beer, which, like most wheat beers, is an acquired taste. This one's taste just takes a little longer to acquire.

Alcohol: 5.0%

The good:
Funky, flavoursome and a conversation starter.

The bad:
The conversation might start with 'What the hell is this?'

Best for:
Quiet contemplation.

Colour, condition & carbonation:
Cloudy golden in colour with good carbonation.

Under the hood:
There are hints of fruit salad, old rego stickers – you name it, you'll probably find it here.

Performance:
The beer has a pleasant grip which cuts through the busyness of flavour and aroma – the overall impression is surprisingly well balanced and the finish relatively clean.

SCORE: 82

BEECHWORTH BLING INDIA PALE ALE

Mega-hopped pale ale in the micro-brewery idiosyncratic style – you either love it or hate it.

Alcohol: 4.8%

The good:
If you really, really like hops, you'll love it.

The bad:
A little too much of a good thing perhaps?

Best for:
Strongly flavoured super salty seafood.

Colour, condition & carbonation:
Dark, cloudy and foreboding, with a real rustic look to it and good carbonation.

Under the hood:
The aroma has lots going on – nuts and honey, as well as green pine smelling hops.

Performance:
In the mouth the hops come to the fore, lining the sides of the mouth while the coffeeish-flavoured malt slips down the middle. The hops leave an aftertaste that hangs and hangs like an opera singer's last note that never ends.

SCORE: 83

BEECHWORTH PALE ALE

Rather rustic, over-hopped pale ale that doesn't quite come together.

Alcohol: 4.8%

The good:
Tastes like the product of a micro-microbrewery.

The bad:
Lacks balance and harmony.

Best for:
Drinking in Beechworth.

Colour, condition & carbonation:
Copper mahogany with low carbonation and cloudiness.

Under the hood:
Estery aroma mixed with herbal notes and something reminiscent of a new pair of rubber-soled shoes in a cardboard box.

Performance:
The hops in this beer are like a manic drummer who keeps hitting cymbals on the off beats. The hops seem to clang in at the wrong moments and make for a bit of a jerky ride.

SCORE: 75

BELLARINE BITTER

Organic, obviously micro-brewed ale that tastes fruity and wholesome.

Alcohol: 5.0%

The good:
It's a micro-brewed natural-tasting ale.

The bad:
The carbonation is a bit odd.

Best for:
Pickled onions.

Colour, condition & carbonation:
Cloudy and teak-coloured in appearance; the bubbles are vigorous and prickly – and a bit too much.

Under the hood:
Soothing chocolatey malt aromas mix with fruity ones. Hopping is a blend of tobacco leaf aromas and rusting steel.

Performance:
It all performs quite well on the palate except the energetic nature of the carbonation, which tends to feel like you're drinking the head of the beer rather than the good stuff below.

SCORE: 82

BELLARINE QUEENSCLIFF ALE

Easy drinking, no-frills, natural-tasting ale that's easy to knock back and grows on you with each sip.

Alcohol: 4.5%

The good:
No nasties, not too fruity.

The bad:
In the company of some of the rambunctious ales in this chapter, it seems a little shy.

Best for:
Drinking by the pint.

Colour, condition & carbonation:
Cloudy, with sudsy head and good carbonation.

Under the hood:
There's the faint nostalgic aroma of the dashboards in 1970s Falcons along with some mealy aromas and a hint of steely hops.

Performance:
Well balanced, not too carbonated and easy to put away, it's a pleasant ale for not thinking drinking.

SCORE: 86

BEER BY THE BAY

QUEENSCLIFF ALE

330ML

BELLARINE THE HEADS ALE

Well-balanced ale with good hopping and intriguing yeast-derived aromas and flavours.

Alcohol: 5.2%

The good:
Aroma, carbonation and aftertaste are all very good.

The bad:
Might be hard to get outside the Bellarine Peninsula.

Best for:
Corned beef sandwiches with pickles.

Colour, condition & carbonation:
Red mahogany with good ale-style head, sudsy lacing and slight cloudiness.

Under the hood:
A pleasant mixture of aromatic and bittering hops not overdone, smoky, almost woody, along with fruit and spice.

Performance:
The bitterness is spot-on, cleaning up this rich ale nicely. This is a finely balanced brew.

SCORE: 90

BLUETONGUE GINGER BEER

An alcoholic ginger beer that works surprisingly well. More alcoholic soft drink than beer.

Alcohol: 4.0%

The good:
It's different.

The bad:
If you want to drink actual beer, this isn't it.

Best for:
Something unusual.

Colour, condition & carbonation:
Golden in colour with good carbonation and head.

Under the hood:
Spicy ginger dominates and definitely more ginger beer, than beer.

Performance:
There are better ginger beers (especially homemade ones) but it's not bad, the balance is okay and it definitely achieves its goals.

SCORE: 80

CASCADE BLONDE

Wheat- and barley-based brew that is light on its feet and well constructed.

Alcohol: 4.8%

The good:
Easy-drinking wheat beer.

The bad:
A bit bland for a wheat beer.

Best for:
Sipping, well chilled, on hot afternoons.

Colour, condition & carbonation:
Yellow gold in colour, good mousse and lacing, and as clear as a lager.

Under the hood:
Spicy green, a hint of fresh coriander, nutmeg and some sweet honey.

Performance:
Slips down easily with little bite or grab – but no lingering nasties. This is a sessional wheat beer.

SCORE: 86

DUKE PALE ALE

Refreshing pale ale stylishly brewed, which isn't so much a massive brewing statement as a decent beer.

Alcohol: 4.8%

The good:
Highly quaffable pale ale that shows its Queensland roots in its ability to be drunk in numbers, in warm climates.

The bad:
A smidgeon more bittering would be better.

Best for:
Freshly peeled lake prawns.

Colour, condition & carbonation:
Copper bronze in colour, with good head and carbonation on the ale side.

Under the hood:
For a boutique beer, the funk factor is low. Aromas of well-applied steely hops and deep malt are integrated nicely – a professional aroma for a boutique beer.

Performance:
With the carbonation low, this is an easy beer to consume. High hop notes mix with the low malt ones nicely and the finish is long and sophisticated.

SCORE: 90

GAGE ROADS INDIA PALE ALE

Western Australian IPA that doesn't have the same charisma as some of its competitors.

Alcohol: 5.1%

The good:
It's a pretty good naturally brewed beer.

The bad:
It lacks a bit of IPA grunt.

Best for:
IPA tastings and comparisons.

Colour, condition & carbonation:
Deep rose-gold in colour, the head goes quickly.

Under the hood:
There are a range of aromas in the glass from banana chips to turtle wax – and the insides of clean fridges.

Performance:
Balance is pretty good, but there's a slight soapiness to the finish where a smidgeon more bittering wouldn't go astray.

SCORE: 86

HOEGAARDEN WITBIER

Legendary wheat beer with the notorious citrus floral wheat beer aromas and funky, mealy look.

Alcohol: 4.9%

The good:
It's a lesson in wheat beer.

The bad:
Don't expect standard lager, this is a different drink.

Best for:
Hot days, chilled down hard.

Colour, condition & carbonation:
Cloudy yellow with good mousse and vigorous, typically efficient, wheat beer foam.

Under the hood:
Yeast and banana bread with spicy orangey notes – it's very distinctive.

Performance:
Clean and fresh, it zips through the mouth surprisingly easily, given the heavy aroma and without lingering esteriness.

SCORE: 91

JAMES SQUIRE GOLDEN ALE

A beer that probably won't get utilised the way it should be. This is a thirst slaker.

Alcohol: 4.5%

The good:
A worthy, hot day alternative to standard lagers.

The bad:
It's not on tap in the local pub.

Best for:
Discerning drinkers.

Colour, condition & carbonation:
Beautiful copper bronze, healthy persistent head, good lacing and mild ale-like carbonation.

Under the hood:
Complexity aplenty here – toasty caramelly malt aromas balanced by some fruitiness and spicy hops, even with mandarin or cumquat notes.

Performance:
Nothing to fault in how this beer rides across the palate. There's a perfect balance of yin and yang in the hops and malt department.

SCORE: 92

JAMES SQUIRE ORIGINAL AMBER ALE

A fruity, aromatic ale with plenty of flavour and kick. Honest and appetising, the way ale should be.

Alcohol: 5.0%

The good:
Loads of character, tastes like you imagine beer used to taste like in Australia in the 1920s (but probably didn't).

The bad:
Doesn't really suit stubby drinking. Pour it into a beer mug.

Best for:
Salt and pepper squid.

Colour, condition & carbonation:
Coppery gold in colour with plenty of carbonation and good lacing.

Under the hood:
There's a little fresh greenery overlaying some roasted vegetable and some banana-like estery characters.

Performance:
There's a real earthy honesty to the flavour and the way this brew travels across the palate. It almost tastes organic, and like most of the James Squire brews, the balance is very good.

SCORE: 88

James Squire Original Amber Ale is a handcrafted blend of Pale and Crystal malts, three distinct hops and a 140-year-old top fermenting ale yeast. Deep copper in colour with a creamy head, this beer rewards the appreciative drinker with a long, slightly nutty finish.

ORIGINAL AMBER ALE

345mL 5.0% ALC/VOL

LITTLE CREATURES BRIGHT ALE

A filtered ale with clarity (hence 'bright'), but with definite Little Creatures hopping.

Alcohol: 4.5%

The good:
Flavour and style.

The bad:
It's a little like an abridged version of the fantastic pale ale.

Best for:
Thai fishcakes.

Colour, condition & carbonation:
Bright, clear and golden with a good rim of bubbles.

Under the hood:
Rich, toasty, treacly malt with a citrus, nutty, floral lift.

Performance:
A generous beer, well constructed, with juicy hops and plenty of tactility in the malt, and it finishes well.

SCORE: 88

LITTLE CREATURES PALE ALE

One of the first of the new breed of pale ales with heaps of hopping and loads of flavour.

Alcohol: 5.2%

The good:
Flavour, power and aroma.

The bad:
Difficult to consume by the six-pack.

Best for:
Pickled octopus.

Colour, condition & carbonation:
Amber, with gentle carbonation and slightly cloudy appearance.

Under the hood:
Those hop aromas leap out of the glass – grapefruit, gewürztraminer, even rose petal overlaying some toasty malt.

Performance:
The edges of this beer are clearly defined by bittering hops. The finish lingers for aeons and it's a beer that really does make you feel like you've drunk something special – it's a classic.

SCORE: 92

LITTLE CREATURES ROGERS' BEER

A unique beer – colour and aroma suggest a winter sipper, but it's surprisingly drinkable and versatile.

Alcohol: 3.8%

The good:
Intriguing, hoppy, paradoxically rich but quaffable at the same time.

The bad:
Love or hate hopping. If you're into hops you'll adore it, if not you'll think they've tipped a bucket too many into the kettle.

Best for:
A quiet one accompanied by a packet of quality salt and vinegar chips.

Colour, condition & carbonation:
The colour of strong tea with sudsy, quickly subsiding head.

Under the hood:
There's some caramelly malt underneath the fruity, citrusy hopping that is a signature of the Little Creatures brewery.

Performance:
Much more mouth-filling than its low alcohol would suggest – the balance of bitterness is excellent, and for a dark beer it finishes clean and doesn't cloy.

SCORE: 90

MATILDA BAY ALPHA PALE ALE

An aficionado's brew that is big on hops and deep on malt. Hop freaks will love it.

Alcohol: 5.2%

The good:
A charismatic love or hate beer. If you love bitter tangy hops, it's for you.

The bad:
If you're a sweet tooth, forget it.

Best for:
Big thirsts that require big flavours.

Colour, condition & carbonation:
Rusty gold colour, with heaps of carbonation and good lacing – this beer looks fresh.

Under the hood:
Sniffing this beer brings back a dim memory of slashing weeds on a tractor in freshly polished boots. Underneath that there's a sweeter aroma of bush honey.

Performance:
This beer launches salvoes against bitterness receptors, while the malt travels a straight path though the middle. It's a beer that features a dénouement and conclusion.

SCORE: 94

MATILDA BAY BEEZ NEEZ

Interesting style of wheat beer with added honey, which has provided a different fermentable sugar.

Alcohol: 4.7%

The good:
Original, quaffable easy-drinking wheat beer.

The bad:
Not that good for quenching.

Best for:
Sipping well chilled.

Colour, condition & carbonation:
Bright honey gold in colour (no joke!), with good bubble and head.

Under the hood:
Grassy hop aromas mix with deeper malt and some sweet floral/honey.

Performance:
Light, not too edgy, this beer goes down easily with minimal fuss with just a hint of mid-palate body.

SCORE: 87

MOO BREW PALE ALE

Quirky take on the pale-ale style, if you like 'em perfumed, you'll like this one.

Alcohol: 4.9%

The good:
It's not short on aroma — this is a beer you can dab behind your ears.

The bad:
It's just a bit flowery.

Best for:
Proustian beer drinking.

Colour, condition & carbonation:
Slightly cloudy red/gold with good bead and head retention.

Under the hood:
Where do I start? Lavender drops, bath salts, Brylcreem, spearmint, new cars, and a male fragrance made in the 1980s called Jazz.

Performance:
It's a pity its just a little over-the-top in the aromatic department, because on the palate, the balance is good — the hops do their bittering work nicely.

SCORE: 83

MOO BREW HEFEWEIZEN WHEAT BEER

Classy wheat beer from a stylish new Tasmanian micro-brewery, with the intrigue of a good wheat beer and not too much funk.

Alcohol: 5.1%

The good:
Easy drinking with plenty of flavour.

The bad:
The shape of the bottle means they don't stack — and can slide out of the fridge and smash.

Best for:
Nori rolls garnished with sesame seeds.

Colour, condition & carbonation:
Pale and quite cloudy with minimum head.

Under the hood:
Interesting aromas of yeast, with hints of citrus in the form of candied peel. It's harmonious and intriguing.

Performance:
Easy to drink and — despite apparent richness and yeastiness — it's also light and refreshing.

SCORE: 90

MOUNTAIN GOAT HIGHTAIL ALE

A tasty, bottle-conditioned ale that adapts nicely to standard Australian beer drinking.

Alcohol: 4.5%

The good:
Appealing, balanced and flavoursome ale, which doesn't weigh you down.

The bad:
Availability – it can be hard to get outside Melbourne.

Best for:
Autumnal beer drinking with fried whitebait.

Colour, condition & carbonation:
The colour of antique furniture, plenty of cloudiness and real ale head.

Under the hood:
Some chocolate-mocha malt is enhanced by whiffs of fresh citrusy hops.

Performance:
The hops kick in early, taming the richness of the malt and keeping things on line right to the very end (and even further) – it's a very well balanced ale.

SCORE: 90

MOUNTAIN GOAT INDIA PALE ALE

A certified organic pale ale that is pale in colour with that signature Mountain Goat drive and thrust.

Alcohol: 5.0%

The good:
It's certified organic and actually tastes like it. It could even be good for you!

The bad:
The carbonation is slightly aggressive when first poured.

Best for:
Hot smoked fish with fresh horseradish.

Colour, condition & carbonation:
The colour of a clover honey, the head is comprised of big bubbles and there's a cloudy haze.

Under the hood:
Nice hop balance going from aromatic – in a spicy, citrusy almost white wine like sense – to bitter, in a smooth transition.

Performance:
The hops are spot-on giving the impression of cleanliness, despite the yeasty fruitiness. The bitterness in the finish is not aggressive but lingers for ages.

SCORE: 88

MOUNTAIN GOAT PALE ALE

Assertive pale ale with plenty of spicy hopping – and no shortage of flavour or yeastiness.

Alcohol: 4.5%

The good:
Tastes like a health tonic as much as a beer.

The bad:
There are some funky estery aromas going on that those wedded to standard brews will find off-putting.

Best for:
Fried salt cod.

Colour, condition & carbonation:
Cloudy, but still bright gold in colour, with excellent carbonation and steady head.

Under the hood:
Where do I start? Whiffs of bowls of oranges that are a little bit past their 'use by' date, mixed with surfboard resin and lemon thyme – in a most attractive way.

Performance:
A nicely balanced pale ale, it slips across the palate with good bitterness and leaves a pleasant lingering sensation.

SCORE: 89

MURRAY'S NIRVANA PALE ALE

A pale ale with plenty of flavour and character — a 'no guts no glory' brew.

Alcohol: 4.5%

The good:
Not shy or bashful in flavour or aroma.

The bad:
Lacks a bit of line and length.

Best for:
Salt and pepper squid.

Colour, condition & carbonation:
Amber coloured, with a touch of copper, not quite clear, with good carbonation and head retention.

Under the hood:
No shortage of stuff going on in the glass — a whiff of freshly cut mango meets freshly mown paspalum and tobacco leaf, along with some toffeeish malt.

Performance:
While the bittering hops grip the sides of the mouth forcefully, the brew lacks a little direction as it heads south. A bit more bittering cohesion wouldn't go astray.

SCORE: 84

MURRAY'S SASSY BLONDE

Belgian-style pale ale with Styrian Goldings hops and an intriguing citric twist to the flavour.

Alcohol: 4.5%

The good:
It's a well-balanced and intriguing ale.

The bad:
Some esoteric fish oil aromas might not be everyone's cup of tea.

Best for:
Fish and chips.

Colour, condition & carbonation:
Bronze with copper tints, spot-on carbonation and low head.

Under the hood:
A bit of orange peel combines with toffee, Bonox or beef stock cube and a hint of fish oil.

Performance:
First impressions are very appealing. Hops tantalise the sides of the mouth and the palate weight is good – but the lingering fish oil flavours are an acquired taste.

SCORE: 87

PEPPERJACK HAND CRAFTED ALE

An hoppy beer notable for the dash of shiraz grape juice added to the kettle.

Alcohol: 4.7%

The good:
Interesting, with a real Matilda Bay hop signature and a hint of grapey sweetness on the finish.

The bad:
The added shiraz isn't really that noticeable.

Best for:
White mould cheeses on rye bread.

Colour, condition & carbonation:
Rusty gold in colour, there's a sudsy look to the head, but it retains bubble well.

Under the hood:
Whiffs of lucerne hay and Cornwell's Extract of Malt blend cohesively with some grapey, muscatty aromas.

Performance:
Initial impressions are of a fairly hop-dominant brew, but it opens up on the tongue with sweetness and finishes with a honeyed afterglow.

SCORE: 89

REDOAK IRISH RED ALE

Intriguing ale, with a pleasant fruitiness and real interest for the beer sniffer.

Alcohol: 4.5%

The good:
An array of unusual aromas sit well, providing interest without offence.

The bad:
The almost wine-like fruity aromas might put lager lovers off.

Best for:
Baccalau.

Colour, condition & carbonation:
Cloudy red–gold with low-level carbonation and not much head.

Under the hood:
An almost wine-like aroma that smells a little like a funky French sauvignon blanc overlays spicy citrus hopping and caramelly malt.

Performance:
Weird – the flavours and aromas in this beer seem odd, but the effect is surprisingly harmonious, and the beer performs well across the palate.

SCORE: 90

REDOAK ORGANIC HEFEWEIZEN

Hefer what? Hefeweizen is Bavarian cloudy wheat beer, which is what this interesting brew is based on. It uses organic malt and organic hops.

Alcohol: 5.0%

The good:
Well put together and interesting brew.

The bad:
It will give the average VB drinker a bit of a fright.

Best for:
Baked Atlantic salmon.

Colour, condition & carbonation:
Very pale and quite clear for a cloudy beer, carbonation is a little Alka-Seltzerish when first poured.

Under the hood:
Underneath a little fermentation pong there's loads of estery aromas that hint at all sorts of glues, spices and banana flavourings, as well as freshly fermented white wine.

Performance:
Spicy and slightly citric on the palate, there's lightness and zip; it's well balanced and finished nicely.

SCORE: 88

REDOAK ORGANIC PALE ALE

Stylish pale ale with impeccable balance, poise and biodynamic, organic credentials.

Alcohol: 4.6%

The good:
Really well made, nicely balanced, boutique pale ale.

The bad:
Availability is limited.

Best for:
Smoked trout.

Colour, condition & carbonation:
Copper bronze with a bit of cloudiness and soapy ale-like head.

Under the hood:
A clever integration of hops and malt. The hops aren't strident but they are very present.

Performance:
Carbonation is good and the ale slips through the hatch leaving the impression of balance and class – with no gaps or holes and no clangy, hoppy afterburn.

SCORE: 91

SMB CHARLOTTE'S HEFEWEIZEN

Funky, fruity wheat beer, which, like most other wheat beers, is a 'love it or hate it' brew.

Alcohol: 4.7%

The good:
It has plenty of character.

The bad:
It's not particularly quenching.

Best for:
Sipping and sniffing.

Colour, condition & carbonation:
Cloudy, pale gold in colour with loosely packed fizzy head.

Under the hood:
Yeasty aroma with hints of old oranges, cooked muffins and some banana skin.

Performance:
Fruity and tactile – it's a wheat beer that feels its way down your throat, though it does cloy a little.

SCORE: 80

SMB RAZORBACK RED ALE

Drinkable, well-balanced ale and one of the better brews to emerge from this brewery.

Alcohol: 4.8%

The good:
Balance, flavour and finish is all good.

The bad:
It probably tastes even better at Thredbo after a day on the piste.

Best for:
Bar snacks, après skiing.

Colour, condition & carbonation:
The colour of very fine engine oil, it has surprising clarity and low-level head.

Under the hood:
Freshly baked sourdough, and Anzac biscuits cooked on a slightly rusty oven tray.

Performance:
Not too heavy and not too light, this brew – to use a hackneyed phrase – tastes just right. It fills the mouth but leaves it clean and invigorated – inviting another sip.

SCORE: 90

ETHANOL

○○○○○○○

CHAPTER FIVE

Human beings are rarely satisfied. Beer is a perfect, mildly alcoholic beverage – but for some, that's not enough. Both amateur and professional brewers persist in trying to make beer what it isn't. Monstrous beers are concocted with the alcohol content of wine, while some go the other way and produce beer with the alcoholic power of a weak shandy.

To many drinkers, light beer is an abomination. It's beer without *cojones*. It's castrated, neutered ale – the liquid equivalent of seedless watermelons and burp-free cucumbers. Veteran drinkers put forward a quite reasonable argument that beer is meant to make you drunk – otherwise you would never know when to stop drinking.

But these arguments aside, beer has always been a servant to society and light beer has a long history of emerging in times of human need. Back in medieval Europe, low-alcohol beer wasn't called 'lite' it was called 'small beer', and was brewed from the dregs of proper, full-strength brews. Its impetus wasn't weight loss or drink driving; it was cholera and other waterborne diseases. Small beer was sterile, hence 'healthy', and was consumed by the bucket load by children and the poorly. The fact that it was mildly alcoholic was neither here nor there.

In the 1920s, when the US was cursed by the plague of prohibition, alcohol-free beer, or 'near beer' as it was known, was invented. It was hugely popular, especially when the alcohol was put back in via a dash of bootleg liquor.

In the 1960s the breath test was introduced, but not without some disquiet. Some drinkers claimed it was their right to drink and drive, others argued that a few drinks actually helped them drive! In various studies, beer was identified as the main culprit when it came to drink driving. So, with the emergence of the 'booze bus', the RBT and breathalysers in clubs and pubs, came 'lite' beer.

Now comes the age of vanity, to which beer has responded by producing low-carb brews. For the vain and the fat, these beers offer the same carbs as light beer (and a third of normal beer) but with standard-grade alcohol content.

Brewing potable light beer is not easy. When yeasts ferment sugar into alcohol, they produce stinky substances known as methional. This pong is mostly hidden in full-strength beer, but shows up once the beer flavour is stripped back. Experiments have proved that the less alcohol in the beer, the more easy it is to detect methional. The task for the brewer is to make light beer that not only tastes full-strength, but doesn't reek. Tricky. That's one of the reasons the mid-strength brew has been so successful: it crosses the divide between light and standard, and has become a staple of those warm northern and western states, where you have to keep drinking beer to remain hydrated.

The light category is now more diverse than ever. From standard lights, which sit at under 3% alcohol, to the mid-strength beers that are near 4%, to the low-carb brews, light has never been better. It's still a compromise, but it's not half as bad as it used to be.

BLUETONGUE PREMIUM LIGHT

Light brew from the Hunter that smells the goods but tastes just a bit too 'light'.

Alcohol: 2.7%

The good:
It's another addition to the choice of light.

The bad:
The light part of it is a bit obvious.

Best for:
Drinking when you really have to watch yourself.

Colour, condition & carbonation:
Dark in colour with some real bronze to the gold, and vigorous bubble.

Under the hood:
Quite a nice aroma of treacle, soaked grain and clean hops.

Performance:
The carbonation is just a bit too fluffy, but that aside, everything is good. The finish is okay, but the main problem is a perceived lack of richness and body – this is the perennial problem with light beer.

SCORE: 85

BOAG'S CLASSIC BLONDE

Boag's take on the low-carb beer, this one offers 475kJ for the 375ml bottle.

Alcohol: 4.5%

The good:
Guilt- and gut-free drinking.

The bad:
Drink Boag's Draught and take some exercise.

Best for:
Weight loss.

Colour, condition & carbonation:
Bronze gold with good head and carbonation.

Under the hood:
A bit of a Pride of Ringwood-ish rusty metal pong on the nose, like classic Australian lagers, overlaying a little sweetness.

Performance:
The carbonation and condition of this beer is very good, but it does have some obvious holes in the mid-palate due to the lack of carbs. It's obvious that you're compromising somewhere.

SCORE: 82

BONDI BLONDE

Low-carb lager brewed by Bluetongue —
delivering only 439kJ per 330ml bottle.

Alcohol: 4.5%

The good:
Well-constructed, easy-
drinking mid-strength brew.

The bad:
Could do with a little bit
more bitterness.

Best for:
Dieting.

**Colour, condition
& carbonation:**
Colour and appearance is
excellent, and carbonation
is good.

Under the hood:
Some warmed honey/malt
aromas and some spice in
the form of ginger on the
nose — and the faintest hint
of steely hops.

Performance:
It's gentle and runs quite
smoothly, while the lack of
carbs is not too apparant.
But in 'true' beer terms (and
quenchability), it lacks a bit
of bitterness.

SCORE: 85

CARLTON MID

This was the beer that set mid-strength beers on their path to glory in the warmer states.

Alcohol: 3.5%

The good:
A pretty good low-alcohol Aussie lager.

The bad:
Finishes slightly empty.

Best for:
Carlton beer drinking for grown-ups.

Colour, condition & carbonation:
A hint of bronze to the colour, and the perfect prickle to the carbonation for thirst quenching.

Under the hood:
Whiffs of sweet malt and CUB hopping remind the drinker that this is of the Carlton family.

Performance:
This beer performs well up until the back straight, when an empty steely taste (akin to sucking on a stainless-steel knife) compels the drinker to take another sip.

SCORE: 85

CASCADE PREMIUM LIGHT

A revelation as far as light beers go – if you have to drink light but want to drink well, this is your brew.

Alcohol: 2.7%

The good:
Good aroma and flavour and the finish is only slightly compromised by the lack of alcohol.

The bad:
For light beer it's hard to fault.

Best for:
Drinking beer for flavour not alcohol.

Colour, condition & carbonation:
Bright rose-gold in colour, tight head, good lacing and plenty of carbonation.

Under the hood:
Exotic, 'premium' nose, clever, grassy, spicy hopping overlaying a little sweet malt.

Performance:
This beer attracts with its aroma – and doesn't detract with its flavour. Good depth and crispness with a slight hole on the back palate (which is unavoidable), but the finish lingers longer than most lights.

SCORE: 90

DUKE MID STRENGTH

One of the first micro-brewery lighter-alcohol beers – and a first-rate effort.

Alcohol: 3.5%

The good:
Quenching, with some definite pilsner character, and the lack of alcohol isn't obvious.

The bad:
None.

Best for:
Responsible drinking.

Colour, condition & carbonation:
Pale yellow gold with excitable carbonation.

Under the hood:
Whiffs of Noble Germanic hops, greenery and raw nuts, all leave a stylish and appealing impression.

Performance:
Carbonation is fluffy, but the beer is well balanced. There's a faint lemony grip to the hops – this is great stuff.

SCORE: 91

EMU DRAFT MIDSTRENGTH

WA beer that falls somewhere between a standard mid-strength and a heavy light. Probably a beer you have to grow up drinking to appreciate.

Alcohol: 3.0%

The good:
It's memorable — something you can't say for a lot of reduced-alcohol beer.

The bad:
It's a bit weird.

Best for:
Drinking in WA.

Colour, condition & carbonation:
Dark amber in colour, the head dies fast.

Under the hood:
There's that classic Emu swampy/rivermouth aroma mixed with something a bit perfumed — like urinal mints or room deodoriser. Underneath all that is a hint of bush honey and some rusty guitar strings.

Performance:
Fairly clunky across the palate, there's a dollop of sweetness followed by some bitterness. It's not ideally balanced.

SCORE: 79

FOSTER'S LIGHT ICE

One of the first light beers and, in an evolutionary sense, a bit like Neanderthal man.

Alcohol: 2.3%

The good:
The alcohol content is very low – you can drink two stubbies of this for every stubby of standard.

The bad:
I'd prefer to drink one stubby of standard than two stubbies of this.

Best for:
Those who don't put much emphasis on taste and balance.

Colour, condition & carbonation:
Dark gold in colour, with good head retention.

Under the hood:
A little bit of CUB-style hopping, sweet and sour, along with a hint of brimstone or sulphur.

Performance:
This is a light beer with a structure that is really affected by the lack of alcohol. It seems to finish halfway through and ends quite soapily.

SCORE: 65

GAGE ROADS PILS MIDSTRENGTH

Finely constructed mid-strength beer with plenty of cut and thrust.

Alcohol: 3.5 %

The good:
A lower alcohol beer that doesn't taste compromised.

The bad:
Not much, it's pretty good.

Best for:
Drinking a few more and staying sensible.

Colour, condition & carbonation:
Gold, with steady head, sticky lacing and good rim of foam.

Under the hood:
Typical Gage Roads – minty, spearmint hops sit over aromas of freshly cooked Anzac biscuits. There's no sense in the aroma that this is mid-strength beer.

Performance:
Well balanced with good, grippy hops, this beer finishes dry and tart, and is a first-rate mid-strength beer.

SCORE: 90

GULF LAGER MID STRENGTH

Rather unappealing Queensland mid-strength beer brewed by Castlemaine Perkins.

Alcohol: 3.2%

The good:
You wouldn't refuse it on a stinking-hot day.

The bad:
Unbalanced bittering.

Best for:
Sipping politely with your Queensland relations.

Colour, condition & carbonation:
Quite a deep bronze, with a tendency for the head to fade fast.

Under the hood:
Whiffs of drains and rusty metal are not particularly enticing.

Performance:
The hops are steely and rather selective in their bittering. The effect is rather disjointed, but the low alcohol content is not hugely apparent.

SCORE: 79

HAHN PREMIUM LIGHT

One of the better light beers — well made and not as big a compromise as it could be.

Alcohol: 2.7%

The good:
Good complexity in the aroma and well made.

The bad:
You still notice that missing couple of per cent.

Best for:
Weeknights.

Colour, condition & carbonation:
Light and bright in colour, with good head retention.

Under the hood:
Nice hopping — a mixture of what seems like Pride of Ringwood and some more exotic hops.

Performance:
This light beer has 0.5% more alcohol than some light beers — and it helps. That and a little bit of sweetness fills out the mid-palate. The beer tastes relatively complete for its low alcohol.

SCORE: 85

JAMES BOAG'S PREMIUM LIGHT

Reeking of Noble hops and with another 0.7% alcohol, it's the thinking pilsner drinker's light beer.

Alcohol: 2.9%

The good:
The hopping is fresh, fragrant and inviting.

The bad:
Something in that exotic hopping makes the subconscious expect a bit more body and alcohol.

Best for:
Quenching quality thirsts.

Colour, condition & carbonation:
Pale gold in colour, with excellent carbonation and head retention.

Under the hood:
Whiffs of Noble German and Czech hops, and nutty malt mix with a grassy freshness – all very nice.

Performance:
Tastes and feels premium until the end, where the lack of alcohol makes its presence felt. As far as light goes, it's one of the best.

SCORE: 92

TOOHEYS MAXIM

A low-cal beer brewed with the very latest technology and, all things considered, it's pretty well done.

Alcohol: 4.6%

The good:
You can drink 20% more beer for the same amount of kilojoules.

The bad:
Are kilojoules what beer drinking is really about? Drink really good beer and eat less bar snacks.

Best for:
Beer drinkers on diets.

Colour, condition & carbonation:
Honey gold in colour, with good head and carbonation – there's nothing wrong with how it looks.

Under the hood:
Surprisingly aromatic in an understated way, with a little bit of hay-like Saaz-ish activity up front – which is all quite appealing in a soft, feminine way.

Performance:
Very easy to throw down – the only sign of those missing carbs is a dead spot just before the finish.

SCORE: 85

VB MIDSTRENGTH LAGER

A challenge to the hegemony XXXX Gold has in Queensland – and a worthy competitor.

Alcohol: 3.5%

The good:
A classic Aussie-tasting lager with less alcohol. One stubby equals one standard drink.

The bad:
If you want to get pissed, you have to drink a hell of a lot of beer.

Best for:
Drinking when responsible for the car, the children, the dog, etc.

Colour, condition & carbonation:
Standard lager colour with a lazy head but sticky lacing.

Under the hood:
Classic CUB hopping, but not as steely or sweet and sour as standard VB – and actually a little more attractive.

Performance:
The first thing that you notice about lower alcohol beers is a lack of balance – but that isn't apparent here until right on the finish. It's a crisp, easy-drinking brew and a worthy addition to the mainstream beerscape.

SCORE: 88

WEST END GOLD

Low-alcohol mid-strength brew which is quite well done.

Alcohol: 3.0%

The good:
Quite well put together mid-strength brew which is 0.5% lower than the average mid-strength beer.

The bad:
It still doesn't measure up to full-strength beer.

Best for:
Port Power vs Adelaide Crows matches.

Colour, condition & carbonation:
With the colour of honey, a good rim of bubbles and lacing, it ticks all the boxes.

Under the hood:
A little bit of cold steel, a hint of mint and a whiff of cooked rice on the nose.

Performance:
For a light/mid brew, this isn't too bad. A tad empty on the mid-palate and in the finish it's a smidgeon soapy, but it does the job of a low-alcohol beer.

SCORE: 85

WEST END LIGHT

A well-made light beer which has quite good balance.

Alcohol: 2.3%

The good:
Nice hopping and good carbonation.

The bad:
Not much – as far as mass-market light beer goes, it's arguably one of the better products.

Best for:
When you want to consume a few – but you still have things to do.

Colour, condition & carbonation:
Amber gold in colour, good head and lacing around the glass that comes from the best tap beer.

Under the hood:
A bit sweet and sour in the hop/malt department, a hint of cooked rice and appealing freshness.

Performance:
Well balanced and easy to knock back, this beer shows just how far light beer has come. There's beer flavour and beer balance without alcohol.

SCORE: 86

XXXX GOLD

Hugely successful mid-strength beer in Queensland. Apparently, for every three beers poured in the Sunshine State, two of them are XXXX Gold.

Alcohol: 3.5%

The good:
It's an easy-drinking mid-strength brew.

The bad:
Lacks a bit of personality and mid-palate oomph.

Best for:
Drinking in Queensland when you don't want to stick out.

Colour, condition & carbonation:
Amber, with a fragile head and good carbonation.

Under the hood:
Steely, slightly sour hops sit above a little whiff of sweet malt – nothing too out of the ordinary here.

Performance:
All goes according to plan and runs smoothly along the rails until after swallowing, when there's the perception that there is something – alcohol – missing.

SCORE: 83

XXXX LIGHT

A light beer that does its job, is quite refreshing and has no nasty flavours.

Alcohol: 2.3%

The good:
Easy drinking at half the alcohol of standard brews.

The bad:
Not bursting with character.

Best for:
Sensible beer drinking in Queensland.

Colour, condition & carbonation:
Dark gold in colour, with good head retention, good lacing and carbonation.

Under the hood:
There's that telltale faintly nutty XXXX aroma and some steely hops, but it's all very polite.

Performance:
The carbonation is good and makes up for the lack of alcohol in the body. All up, the beer is quite well put together, although it does finish a bit watery.

SCORE: 85

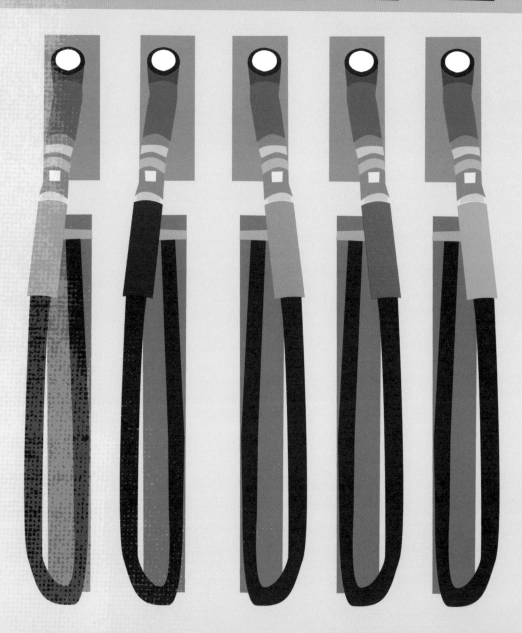

INDEX

ACKNOWLEDGMENTS

Thanks to my beloved wife and kids for looking benevolently on a husband/father who would start drinking at 9.00am every morning; to the local tip for recycling the empties; to my dishwasher for washing up all those glasses; to all the people involved at Murdoch Books for their patience; and to my liver for standing up to the task.

Published in 2008 by Murdoch Books Pty Limited

Murdoch Books Australia
Pier 8/9, 23 Hickson Road
Millers Point NSW 2000
Phone: +61 (0) 2 8220 2000
Fax: +61 (0) 2 8220 2558
www.murdochbooks.com.au

Murdoch Books UK Limited
Erico House, 6th Floor
93–99 Upper Richmond Road
Putney, London SW15 2TG
Phone: +44 (0) 20 8785 5995
Fax: +44 (0) 20 8785 5985
www.murdochbooks.co.uk

Chief Executive: Juliet Rogers
Publishing Director: Kay Scarlett

Project Manager: Emma Hutchinson
Editor: Paul McNally
Design Concept and Layout: Hugh Ford
Illustrations: Hugh Ford
Photography: Brett Stevens
Production: Kita George

National Library of Australia Cataloguing-in-Publication Data:
Powell, Greg Duncan
Beer : a gauge for enthusiasts
Includes index.
ISBN 978 1 741962 109 (pbk.)
Beer – Guidebooks.
Breweries – Guidebooks.
Beer – Flavor and odor.
Non-alcoholic beer.
641.23

Printed by Imago in 2008
PRINTED IN CHINA.